**YELLOWSTONE
TO YUKON**

This edition belongs to...

YELLOWSTONE
_TO_ YUKON

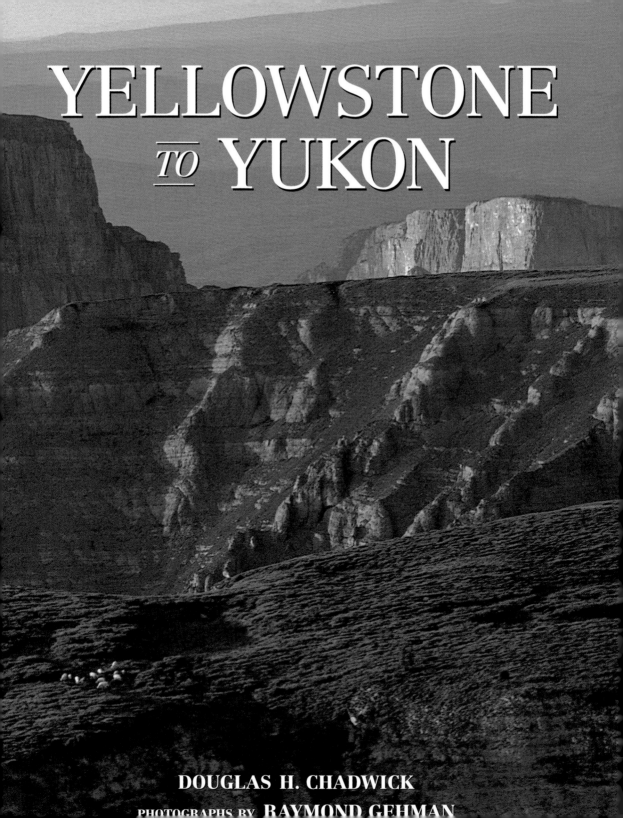

YELLOWSTONE
_TO_ YUKON

DOUGLAS H. CHADWICK

PHOTOGRAPHS BY **RAYMOND GEHMAN**

CONTENTS

Destined for high places from birth, a lone mountain goat stands vigil over the crown of the continent, the Rocky Mountains, on supple hooves with traction soles. PAGE 1: **Striking apostrophe** to an evening rainstorm, a rainbow graces the forests of Stone Mountain Provincial Park, B.C., near the Alaska Highway. PAGES 2-3: **Sculptured karstlands** of the Ram Plateau dwarf a scattering of Dall's sheep in North Nahanni country, N.W.T.

Copyright notice and Library of Congress CIP data appear on page 200.

Yukon

Fairbanks.

A L A S K A

② 2

WILD HEART OF A CONTINENT...

Transcending political and bureaucratic boundaries, the vast
ecoregion known as Yellowstone to Yukon—Y2Y—takes in
nearly half a million square miles of Rocky Mountain real estate,
from Wyoming's Yellowstone National Park to the Peel River
of Yukon Territory. It includes 11 national parks, scores of
wilderness areas, state and provincial parks, and other reserves.
Also, Y2Y boasts one of the most intact collections of wildlife
in the world, encompassing both megafauna—such as grizzly
and black bears, bison, elk, moose, wolves and coyotes,
mountain goats and sheep—and a variety of smaller creatures.
The Y2Y Conservation Initiative seeks to preserve this
biogeographical region's unique beauty and natural diversity
by finding ways for human activities to blossom here without
overwhelming nature and the overall quality of life.

Legend

- Yellowstone to Yukon Ecoregion
- National Forest .... N.F.
  Forest Reserve
- National Park .... N.P.
  National Park Reserve
- National Wildlife Refuge ..... N.W.R.
  National Wildlife Area
  Game Reserve
- Indian Reservation .... I.R.
  Indian Reserve
- Provincial Park .... P.P.
  Recreation Area .... R.A.
- Wilderness
- Management Area
- 90 U.S. Interstate Highway
- 2 State Highway
- Trans-Canada Highway
- 97 Canadian Provincial Highway
- ·········· Continental Divide
- □ Point of Interest

UNITED STATES
CANADA

Inuvik

8

ARCTIC CIRCLE

NUNAVUT

NORTHWEST

Great
Bear
Lake

Ogilvie
Mountains
Tombstone
Range
Dawson
Klondike R.
Klondike Hwy.
Stewart
MCARTHUR
WILDLIFE
SANCTUARY

Peel
Wind
Snake
Bonnet Plume
PEEL RIVER
PRESERVE

Mackenzie

TERRITORIES

Yellowknife

YUKON
TERRITORY

Pelly Mts.
Continental
Divide
N. Nahanni
S. Nahanni
Ram
Plateau

Fort
Simpson

2
Yukon
Teslin
Nisutlin
Pelly
Wolf Lake
Mackenzie Mountains
Ram
River
NAHANNI
N.P. RESERVE

Great
Slave
Lake

1
Klondike
River
Whitehorse

Teslin
NISUTLIN RIVER
DELTA NATIONAL
WILDLIFE AREA

Teslin
Lake
Watson
Lake
Scoop Lake Ranch
Liard
STONE MT. P.P.
WOKKPASH R.A.

Peace

Juneau

Stikine Range
Cassiar Mts.
Dease
Lake
DENETIAH P.P.
SPATSIZI
PLATEAU
WILDERNESS
P.P.
TATLATUI P.P.
KWADACHA WILDERNESS P.P.
Stikine
Gataga
River
Kechika
MUNCHO
LAKE
P.P.
MUSKWA-KECHIKA
NORTHERN ROCKY MTS.
P.P.
MANAGEMENT
AREA
ALASKA
HWY.
97
Prophet River
Fort Nelson

ALBERTA

SASKATCHEWAN

37
Continental
Divide
Muskwa Ranges
Rocky Mountain Trench
Williston
Lake
Mackenzie
Chetwynd
C
R
O
C
K
Dawson
Creek
43
Athabasca
N. Saskatchewan

Prince
Rupert

16
KAKWA P.P.
Smoky
WILLMORE
WILDERNESS P.P.
EDMONTON
Saskatoon

Queen
Charlotte
Islands

BRITISH

COLUMBIA

Prince George
16
Fraser
MT. ROBSON P.P.
JASPER N.P.
ROCKY
2
South
Saskatchewan

Columbia Mountains
Fraser
97
WELLS GRAY
P.P.
YOHO N.P.
BANFF
N.P.
MOUNTAINS
FOREST RESERVE
MT. ASSINIBOINE P.P.
Canmore
CALGARY
Bow
M
GLACIER N.P.
MT. REVELSTOKE N.P.
Revelstoke
PURCELL WILDERNESS
CONSERVANCY P.P.
Kelowna
VALHALLA P.P.
KOOTENAY
N.P.
Kananaskis Valley
2
Oldman

Vancouver
Island
VANCOUVER
5
Cranbrook
WATERTON
LAKES N.P.
CANADA
UNITED STATES
15

Victoria

Columbia Mountains
Rocky Mountain Trench
GLACIER
N.P.
GREAT BEAR WILDERNESS
BOB MARSHALL WILDERNESS
Fort Benton
Missouri

PACIFIC

OCEAN

SEATTLE
WASHINGTON
CABINET MTS.
WILDERNESS
FLATHEAD
I.R.
Freezout Lake W.M.A.
MONTANA

Olympia
90
Clearwater
River
Missoula
Helena

82
Snake
Columbia
Portland
84
Salem
5

OREGON

SAWTOOTH
WILDERNESS
Salmon
Bitterroot Range
SELWAY-
BITTERROOT
WILDERNESS
Bitterroot
Valley
FRANK
CHURCH-
RIVER OF
NO RETURN
WILDERNESS
RED ROCK
LAKES
N.W.R.
Henrys Fork
Bozeman
90
Yellowstone

IDAHO
GRAND
TETON
N.P.
YELLOWSTONE
N.P.
SHOSHONE
N.F.
NAT. ELK REFUGE
Gannett Peak
13,804 ft
BRIDGER-
TETON
N.F.
WYO.

Boise
5
86
84
15
Snake

Great
Salt
Lake

CALIF.
NEVADA
UTAH
Green

| 0 | miles | 200 |
| 0 | kilometers | 300 |

Lambert Equal-Area Projection

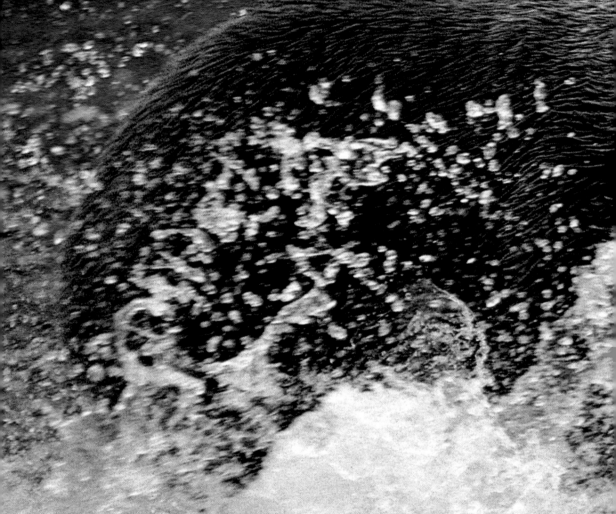

THE VISION

OPPOSITE:

**MUSKWA-KECHIKA,
BRITISH COLUMBIA**

With best friend
Webster to share the
load, Karsten Heuer
nears one of the 100
mountain passes he
crossed during a two-
year, 2,100-mile trek
north from Wyoming
along the Continental
Divide. The former
Canadian park warden
undertook the solo
journey to publicize the
Yellowstone to Yukon
Conservation Initiative.

FOLLOWING PAGES:

**FREEZOUT LAKE
WILDLIFE
MANAGEMENT
AREA, MONTANA**

Like a late winter
storm off the peaks,
snow geese settle onto
stubbled grain fields in
early April. As many as
300,000 geese and
10,000 tundra swans
follow the Rocky
Mountain Front during
their seasonal journeys
north and south.

Extending more than half the length of the northern hemisphere, the Rocky Mountains harbor cacti in their southern portion and tree-less tundra toward their arctic end. But between west-central Wyoming and the northern Mackenzie Mountains of the Yukon Territory, the Rockies have a similar look and feel. Cold, clear, freshly made rivers and winds sweep down from skylines of ice-cut stone while evergreen forests sweep back up from the floodplains to the tundra meadows of the alpine zone. These are montane and boreal, or northern, forests, dominated by a mixture of spruce, fir, pine, and other conifers. Aspen, poplar, and birch line the waterways and wetlands. Snows begin falling on their branches as early as the beginning of autumn and linger into May or June. Yet summers can be warm and at times downright hot. Not long after avalanches are done striping the woodlands, wildfire becomes the major source of variation and renewal for plant com-munities throughout the region.

In the forests' fragrant depths, on the grassy meadows and burned patches, and picking their way across the slide chutes, talus slopes, and rock outcroppings are an extraordinary collection of big, brawny animals from bears to bighorns. Megafauna. Their populations are fairly continuous from north to south, and, together with those of smaller mountain-dwellers, add up to one of the most intact assem-blages of wildlife left anywhere in the world.

Given the scale of the setting and of the creatures that animate it, this is the stronghold—the core of North America's untamed majesty, a place where any young person can set out into bold land-scapes and discover more freedoms than he or she ever imagined the world might hold. It may even be large enough to hold dreams of a lasting frontier. Just how large is that?

On a different journey almost 1,500 miles south of Nahanni coun-try, in Yellowstone National Park, I am still among mountains where winter temperatures sink to -40 or even -50 degrees F. And I am still among wolves. But it is April now. Mountain bluebirds flit like shards of a midsummer sky past the shrinking snowbanks, and the wolves are in a grove of budding aspen. They are arguing with a mother grizzly and her two yearling cubs over the carcass of an elk. My guess is that the pack of five wolves took down the elk, since the site is part of their regular hunting territory, and the bears, recently emerged from their winter den, sniffed out the meat and laid claim to it.

Looking on through a telescope from a granite knoll, I see the wolves circling the grizzlies, coiling steadily closer. All at once, the silver-tipped mother bear wheels and rushes at the closest canine. The cubs race close at her heels to avoid becoming separated and suddenly vulnerable. Wolves scatter in every direction, then regroup to approach again. The same scene plays out several more times before a couple of the younger wolves lie down on the sunlit slope above the carcass to

I love these Rocky Mountains—every skyward one of them, from northern Mexico to where the Brooks Range curves along Alaska's northern rim to overlook the polar sea. I can hardly imagine my own existence separately. Growing up at the Rockies' western edge, I got to know the high country by tagging along each summer behind my geologist father. Besides him, my heroes were mountain men like Jim Bridger and explorers like the Scotsman Alexander Mackenzie. In 1789, Mackenzie ventured to the Arctic Ocean via the mighty, north-flowing river that now bears his name. Then, in 1793, he crossed the Rockies to reach the Pacific coast of British Columbia. Though it's almost unpatriotic for an American to point this out, his northern traverse of the continent—the first recorded crossing by a white man—took place more than a decade before the celebrated team of Lewis and Clark ever left the dock at St. Louis.

As a young man, I went deeper into the Rockies for seasonal work, then moved to take up life among their contours and become a wildlife biologist. My first date with my wife-to-be was a camping trip near the Continental Divide. Tramping across crusted snow to watch the mountain goats I had been studying, we met a wolverine that insisted on following along like some feral chaperone, a behavior I have never seen or heard of in a wolverine since. We married in the mountains, and we settled in a riverside cabin on the western slope within sight of the great divide.

Somewhere in all this, I have the eastward-spreading Pacific seafloor to thank. For the past 175 million years, it has been pushing hard against North America, wrinkling that side of the continent into a roughly parallel series of mountain ranges that run north to south. Geologists lump them together as the western cordillera. Think of it as a work in progress, because the seafloor has not stopped shoving. Some summits are still adding a few inches of height per human life span.

The longest, most massive chain builds along the cordillera's eastern flank, towering over the edge of the great plains like a weather front. That chain is the Rockies. The southern Blackfeet knew these mountains as *Mistakis*—Backbone of the World. Here, where the ground to which humans are bound soars into the realm of the sky, thunder gave people the gift of medicine pipes. A skin-wrapped bundle of plants and animal parts steeped in sacred powers is still opened in a special ritual each spring, as thunder strides back into this country.

Although few whites recognize the name Mistakis, many describe the Rockies as North America's backbone. Windmaker, cloud-snagger, snow-collector, it is the spine from which the continent's waters flow either back toward the Pacific, eastward to the Atlantic, or—beginning where the mountain called Snow Dome rises from the Columbia Icefield in Canada's Jasper National Park—northward into the Arctic Ocean.

Extending more than half the length of the northern hemisphere, the Rocky Mountains harbor cacti in their southern portion and tree-less tundra toward their arctic end. But between west-central Wyoming and the northern Mackenzie Mountains of the Yukon Territory, the Rockies have a similar look and feel. Cold, clear, freshly made rivers and winds sweep down from skylines of ice-cut stone while evergreen forests sweep back up from the floodplains to the tundra meadows of the alpine zone. These are montane and boreal, or northern, forests, dominated by a mixture of spruce, fir, pine, and other conifers. Aspen, poplar, and birch line the waterways and wetlands. Snows begin falling on their branches as early as the beginning of autumn and linger into May or June. Yet summers can be warm and at times downright hot. Not long after avalanches are done striping the woodlands, wildfire becomes the major source of variation and renewal for plant communities throughout the region.

In the forests' fragrant depths, on the grassy meadows and burned patches, and picking their way across the slide chutes, talus slopes, and rock outcroppings are an extraordinary collection of big, brawny animals from bears to bighorns. Megafauna. Their populations are fairly continuous from north to south, and, together with those of smaller mountain-dwellers, add up to one of the most intact assemblages of wildlife left anywhere in the world.

Given the scale of the setting and of the creatures that animate it, this is the stronghold—the core of North America's untamed majesty, a place where any young person can set out into bold landscapes and discover more freedoms than he or she ever imagined the world might hold. It may even be large enough to hold dreams of a lasting frontier. Just how large is that?

On a different journey almost 1,500 miles south of Nahanni country, in Yellowstone National Park, I am still among mountains where winter temperatures sink to -40 or even -50 degrees F. And I am still among wolves. But it is April now. Mountain bluebirds flit like shards of a midsummer sky past the shrinking snowbanks, and the wolves are in a grove of budding aspen. They are arguing with a mother grizzly and her two yearling cubs over the carcass of an elk. My guess is that the pack of five wolves took down the elk, since the site is part of their regular hunting territory, and the bears, recently emerged from their winter den, sniffed out the meat and laid claim to it.

Looking on through a telescope from a granite knoll, I see the wolves circling the grizzlies, coiling steadily closer. All at once, the silver-tipped mother bear wheels and rushes at the closest canine. The cubs race close at her heels to avoid becoming separated and suddenly vulnerable. Wolves scatter in every direction, then regroup to approach again. The same scene plays out several more times before a couple of the younger wolves lie down on the sunlit slope above the carcass to

TED WOOD

THE VISION

PREVIOUS PAGES:

MACKENZIE RIVER, NORTHWEST TERRITORIES

Going against the current of development, the grizzly is hard-pressed to find room in the modern world. Because great bears need habitats like themselves— huge, strong, wild, and part of a still greater whole, efforts to save this threatened species have spurred conservationists and others to look beyond the boundaries of scattered reserves and focus on ways to link remaining wildlands across entire ecosystems.

THE EARTH is bigger here than in most places. It has more surface area in a square mile, more different altitudes and angles, more possibilities to explore—for peaks rise over both shoulders wherever you turn. The easiest path through this terrain is one worn by water, the South Nahanni River. Its course defines 1,840-square-mile Nahanni National Park in Canada's Northwest Territories. Frozen now, the channel looks as hard and white as the surrounding jumble of the Mackenzie Mountains. But currents twisting under the ice have left sections of it treacherously thin.

Cross-country skis help distribute my weight as I travel downriver, and I'm roped to a partner. Better yet, a herd of woodland caribou have gone before us on one long stretch; knowing they weigh far more than either of us, we put our trust in the path they picked over the ice. For miles at a time, the broad crescents of caribou hoofprints are overlain by wolf tracks. A lot of wolf tracks. Packs in this region are often large, mainly because they have to contend with big, tough prey—moose and occasional bison, along with the caribou.

Each day that we travel surrounded by nothing but wildness, the world seems to stand forth more clearly, pared down to strong elements and old truths. There are the hunters and the hunted. Wind. Stone. Forest. The bends of the river and our human curiosity to see what lies around the next one. The snow is dry and powdery, the cold constant. Where the late winter sun reaches through gaps in the mountain walls, raising the temperature to all of 15 degrees F, it feels almost hot as we glide on toward the food cache that waits a few camps ahead. At night, spruce trees pop and crack in the subzero air as northern lights arc between rock spires while wolf songs carry faintly on the breeze from somewhere far down a side canyon.

Dragging wood toward the fire, I cross tracks of ptarmigan or grouse, now probably huddled down for the night in the insulating snowpack. More shadow marks reveal where some little rodent scrambled out of starlit crystals and dove back into them. I press close to the flames a while, then lean away to watch the aurora fluoresce among glittering stars. And I envision, whirling through those depths of space, a partly frozen, blue-and-white sphere bearing a multitude of forms that swim and fly and crawl and prance and rage and play and yearn. It is one thing to say that this living world we share is miraculous. It is another to sense it deep in your bones.

simply keep watch. A few minutes later, the grizzlies' only competition comes from half a dozen ravens hopping on the ground just beyond paw-swipe range, maneuvering to snatch leftovers as a bald eagle hang-glides in to perch on a nearby snag and wait for a chance of its own. In America's and the world's first national park, catching meat and keeping meat can be two very different things.

This famed reserve at the juncture of Idaho, Montana, and Wyoming is close to where the stronghold of boreal forest and mountain megafauna tapers off—or begins, depending upon your perspective. Americans in the lower 48 states tend to think of the snow-capped heights marching from here into Canada as the northern Rockies. Canadians don't, nor do Alaskans. To them, places such as Yellowstone and nearby Grand Teton National Park (at about the same latitude as Iowa cornfields) are anything but northern. A more recent name for the continent's wild core is beginning to be heard: Yellowstone to Yukon. It's fairer. It's more focused. The words beckon, implying a journey. And the abbreviation is catchy in its own right: Y2Y.

From near Riverton, Wyoming, to the Peel River at the northern end of the Mackenzie Mountains, within 40 miles of the Arctic Circle, this ecoregion extends almost 2,000 linear miles and spans almost half a million square miles. Most of it lies above 3,500 feet. The pinnacle is 13,804-foot-high Gannett Peak in Wyoming's Wind River Range. Grand Teton, shining across the Snake River, is second at 13,771 feet. Forests cover almost 60 percent of Y2Y, tundra and bare rock more than 20 percent, and agriculture less than 3 percent. Much of its eastern edge is defined by where it meets the prairie foothills. In contrast, mountains west of the Continental Divide thrust up all the way to the Pacific; here the border of the Y2Y ecoregion is more arbitrary, gradually giving way to coastal influences such as heavier rainfall, higher humidity, warmer winter temperatures, and denser vegetation.

Like a great many people, I once thought of the core of the Rockies largely in terms of its spectacular national parks. I was familiar with Grand Teton, Yellowstone, and Glacier in the U.S.; also with Glacier's sister park, Waterton Lakes, just across the international line, and Banff and Jasper farther north. But I'd never visited the "other" Glacier National Park, in British Columbia. Nor had I been to Kootenay or Mount Revelstoke National Parks, also in Canada. Just thinking of such places made my feet more and more restless.

Currently, 11 national parks occur within the Yellowstone to Yukon ecoregion, 62 percent of which is in Canada. They are joined by an array of designated wilderness areas: Montana's Great Bear, Valhalla in B.C., Alberta's Willmore Wilderness Provincial Park (linked to the north end of Jasper National Park) and enough other wildlands to improve the leg-muscle-to-body-fat-ratio of any North American citizen. Scattered among these are all sizes and shapes of state and provincial parks, recreational areas, wildlife refuges, and forest reserves. Y2Y also takes in all or part of the traditional territories of 31 native North American tribes.

I had always assumed that I knew the Rockies pretty well—until I began staring at the atlas with Y2Y in mind. That's when I had to admit that I was wrong—so wrong that I soon had to face up to some very serious personal issues. Yup. Like, would my favorite old hiking boots hold together for the burst of rambles I was planning, or was I going to have to spring for a new pair? What about upgrading the sleeping bag, another longtime companion and abettor of memories? While I was at it, how was my supply of insect repellent? If you don't think my personal well-being was on the line here, try running out of bug dope while canoeing a northern marsh some sultry July evening.

I would soon learn that Yellowstone to Yukon is a hard-working label with several purposes. One is to draw attention to a special part of the world and encourage people to get to know it better; obviously that has succeeded with me. Secondly, the name emphasizes that this is not merely a geographic area but a biogeographic one that transcends borders between states and provinces and even nations. A third purpose is to spur discussion of how we ought to go about protecting the landscapes and natural resources within such a unique ecoregion. Rugged topography may have kept the smoke and clang and asphalt sprawl of the modern world at bay so far, but this place isn't going to withstand industrial technology combined with soaring population pressures much longer. Not without help.

Finally, there is the Yellowstone to Yukon Conservation Initiative, which is both a movement to promote the beauty, environmental health, and natural diversity of the region and the name of a group. Formed during the mid-1990s, this "group" is actually a network of more than 120 conservation-minded organizations, from local guide and outfitter societies to international heavyweights such as the World Wildlife Fund. Working out of a central office in Canmore, Alberta, just east of Banff National Park, a small staff coordinates projects that include mapping wildlife ranges and other biological resources, economic studies, and research on public opinions.

Contrary to what you might expect, an important part of the Y2Y conservation vision is that it does NOT seek to ban further development and turn much of the region into some sort of superpark. Rather, the idea is to figure out how to proceed with human activities so that, for once, they don't overwhelm other aspects of the ecosystem that contribute to the overall quality of life. Put more simply, the challenge is to discover how to work and play on this land without messing it up. There is no shortage of talk these days about blending the needs of human and wildlife communities. Yellowstone to Yukon is a way of saying: All right. Here is the space and opportunity. It's time to get serious. In the words of initiative coordinator Bart Robinson, "Y2Y represents the best chance anywhere on Earth today to ensure the survival of a functioning mountain ecosystem."

Supporters of the Yellowstone to Yukon Conservation Initiative are motivated by a strong sense of urgency, but they understand that a chief ingredient for success is public education, a process that requires a good deal of patience and time. "This is a hundred-year project," Robinson told me when we first met, in 1997. "We're in year two."

Drawing up detailed plans on the scale to which Y2Y invites us has never been done before. Just trying to do so will be an unprecedented experiment, one that might never have begun were it not for the kinds of snarling wildlife I saw that day in the Yellowstone aspen grove. Large carnivores radiate strength, which demands our attention. But what holds our interest is their undeniable intelligence. We see a good deal of ourselves in such hunters, and more than a little of them in us. Which is probably why they have won lead roles in our stories, myths, and religions since prehistoric times. Even where we've eliminated such beasts, we slap their names and images on everything from automobiles and sports teams to time-share condominiums, hoping to borrow a bit of that top-mammal charisma. Welcome to Bear Meadows Estates.

The brown bear, *Ursus arctos*, is found across much of the Northern Hemisphere. Grizzlies belong to the subspecies *horribilis*, which once ranged throughout most of western North America. These giants are members of the Order Carnivora, complete with the kind of fangs and claws that inspire bad movie scripts. Behaviorally, though, they are omnivores, and very adept ones. They dig for starchy roots, graze sprouting grasses and succulent herbs, munch seeds, nuts, and berries, and lap up insects as well as chase prey the size of moose. They are expert scavengers too, guided by a legendarily keen sense of smell. Animal remains can provide a crucial nutritional boost when, after passing half the year in dens without eating, the bears emerge into landscapes still awaiting the onset of spring growth. While the presence of wolves and cougars means more competition for live prey, it can also translate into having more carcasses around to scavenge.

Grizzlies take over the groceries of much smaller neighbors too. Squirrels, for example. From central British Columbia south, well-drained ridges near timberline favor the growth of whitebark pines. Indians used to travel into these mountains during late summer to gather seeds from the cones. Rich in oils and protein, pine seeds are a staple food for red squirrels, which hoard the bounty in handy crevices or bury piles in the ground. The caches become an invaluable food source for grizzlies especially in autumn, when each day is a race to build up enough fat reserves to outlast another long winter.

Clark's nutcrackers also sock away whitebark pine seeds for the cold months. A single bird may stash between 20,000 and 35,000 seeds in more than a thousand caches, mostly on south-facing slopes where direct sunlight keeps snows from accumulating. Through experiments, scientists have found that this member of the crow and jay family maintains a precise map in its head of its myriad earthen caches, keying them to minor landmarks such as prominent stones or tree snags. It is an impressive display of mental abilities, causing me to wonder if people (like me) who manage to misplace the car keys or checkbook every few days shouldn't swear off using the term birdbrain as a slur.

Nutcracker stores are generally too small to amount to more than an occasional snack for a several-hundred-pound grizz. Yet they are extremely important to the bears as future whitebark plantations. Remarkable as a nutcracker's skill at recall may be, it isn't foolproof. Some stashes always get drifted over by quirky snowstorms, hidden by rock slides, or just plain forgotten. After the thaw, they germinate into fresh crops of seedlings across the mountain slopes. Thus, the welfare of great bears is linked to memory lapses by birdbrains—ah, I mean avian intellects—and to the industry of chittering squirrels as well as to cycles of climate, wildfire, and disease that affect whitebark pine populations, and to the hunting skills of other major predators.

THE QUESTS for living space and nutrients by members of a wildlife community are like ripples in a pond that spread and intersect in endless combinations. Apex predators make especially big waves; the loss of a single species among them can realign patterns throughout an ecosystem. Once reviled as destructive, predators actually help keep prey healthy over time and better fit to cope with the demands of their physical environment. Ecologists realized all this some time ago. More recently, they have begun to appreciate large carnivores even more, as creatures that help maintain biological diversity. If, for example, you live in the eastern U.S. and are alarmed by the decline of songbirds, you might want to consider which missing predators once kept a lid on the likes of raccoons, skunks, and opossums—which are more abundant than ever and take a heavy toll on bird eggs and young.

Wolves are particularly hard on their closest canine competitors, coyotes, often killing them. But where wolves thrive, they improve the prospects for the coyotes' closest canine competitors, the foxes. Together with martens and weasels and other modest-size carnivores, foxes take small but abundant prey such as rodents, whose numbers affect the distribution of seeds and insects—elements that influence the habitats of deer, bighorn sheep, elk, bison, and the rest of the hooved animals hunted by wolves and cougars and scavenged by bears.

Although people talk about the balance of nature all the time, even scientists have a long way to go yet in terms of truly grasping it. Yellowstone, like portions of the Rockies farther north, offers a splendid outdoor laboratory in which to chase answers. That wasn't the case until fairly recently, in part because the last wolf was trapped out of the reserve in 1926. For many years thereafter, government policy continued to favor the obliteration of major predators. An exception was made for bears. In fact, Yellowstone was renowned as the spot to see batches of them. Black bears were a regular feature along roadsides, cadging treats from motoring tourists, and the grizzlies gathered in growly throngs at park garbage dumps, providing a spectacle that rivaled Old Faithful geyser in popularity.

By the 1970s, however, the silver-tipped stars of Yellowstone's wildlife show were in trouble. Officials had banned the feeding of bears and abruptly sealed off all garbage in an effort to improve public safety and restore natural patterns. Those actions had almost exactly the opposite effect at first. Trained over generations to associate food with the presence of humans, grizzlies fanned out from the park to begin raiding garbage and livestock in inhabited areas.

What had been seen as adorable panhandlers were now viewed as problems. Bruins gone wrong. Bad news bears. Authorities set about eliminating troublemakers both in and around the reserve. Combined with ongoing bear hunting seasons in neighboring states, the purge soon reduced Yellowstone's grizzlies to somewhere between around 150 and 300, a total that included perhaps no more than 30 breeding females. That left fewer than 1,000 grizz south of Canada, and in 1975, *Ursus arctos horribilis* was listed as a threatened species in the lower 48 states.

Slightly earlier, during the 1960s, two leading theorists in the field of ecology, E.O. Wilson and Robert MacArthur, were tallying animal populations on oceanic islands. Distant islands tend to have fewer species than those closer to a mainland, they found, and small islands have significantly fewer species than large ones. Depending upon a particular creature's body size and social traits such as territoriality, an island can only hold so many individuals. Low population levels encourage inbreeding; shrinking gene pools decrease survivability of species over time. Island-dwelling animals also can be knocked down by tsunamis, hurricanes, severe droughts, fires, or disease epidemics. Such catastrophes may be rare in a given life span but are inevitable over the centuries, and islands offer little or no room for escape.

The smaller the island, the more likely that the disappearance of one of its life forms will strongly affect others, leading to further losses. For instance, the fruit bats that inhabit certain South Pacific islands are the primary pollinators and distributors of seeds for many key tropical trees. Lose one bat species and whole sections of the forest may dwindle, along with the birds, reptiles, amphibians, and invertebrates that depend upon that particular mix of vegetation. The more isolated an island is, the harder it will be for new species to reach it and swing the pendulum back, toward greater variety and stability.

Such principles of island biogeography apply as well to isolated habitats on the continents. Mountaintops in the American Southwest would be one obvious example, since these relatively cool, moist peaks are basically islands sticking out of a desert sea. Another example turns out to be reserves surrounded by human activities. Wildlife inventories have shown that national parks, from Mount Rainier in Washington to Zion in Utah, have lost an assortment of mammals since they were established—despite full government protection. Large carnivores usually vanish first. As with Yellowstone and its grizzlies, many of these reserves can't sustain viable wildlife populations by themselves. When the animals move beyond park borders, they run out of suitable habitats, food supplies, or the kind of security they require, and eventually wind up dead.

Much of Yellowstone Park consists of snowy mountains and plateaus between one and two miles above sea level. They serve bears as refuges from hunting, poaching, and large-scale development. But for at least part of each year, the terrain within neighboring national forests, federal rangelands, and state lands offers higher quality bear habitat—lush river bottoms, low elevation hillsides that green up earlier in spring, broad berry patches, alpine cirques with insect congregations, and so on.

John and Frank Craighead, the twins who pioneered grizzly bear research, found that Yellowstone's grizzlies wander home ranges as large as several hundred to a thousand square miles. The brothers suggested that the arbitrary boundaries of the park do not enclose enough territory or natural food to ensure grizzly survival.

New research sparked by Yellowstone's sudden decline of bears confirmed the Craigheads' findings. Resource experts realized that it was not fair to hold the National Park Service alone responsible for the animals' welfare. Success was going to require a team effort. Various federal and state agencies would have to coordinate management of natural resources at a level seldom, if ever, practiced before. At the same time, they needed to give equal attention to educating recreationists, landowners, and local communities about how to avoid conflicts with bears.

Like it or not, old habits had to change. Folks needed to clean up after themselves. Take the dog food off the porch. Bury livestock carcasses before they lured bears to the pastures. Hang camp food away from the tent. And generally get better at sharing the countryside with another canny, long-lived, dominant mammal. As the process went forward, people began to talk less and less about just Yellowstone Park and more and more about what came to be called the Greater Yellowstone Ecosystem, a chunk of the Rockies usually described as between 15 and 20 million acres—many times the size of the 2.2 million-acre national park.

FOLLOWING PAGES:
BOW VALLEY, ALBERTA
Life at the crossroads: Tracks of wildlife and wildlife researchers merge with the steel rails of the Canadian Pacific Railway in Alberta's snowbound Banff National Park. Banff's Bow Valley provides crucial winter and spring range for numerous species. But the same bottomlands also host the Trans-Canada Highway and other roadways, as well as the nation's main railroad line. Biologists continue to study ways to reduce the heavy toll that cars and trains take on the area's wild residents.

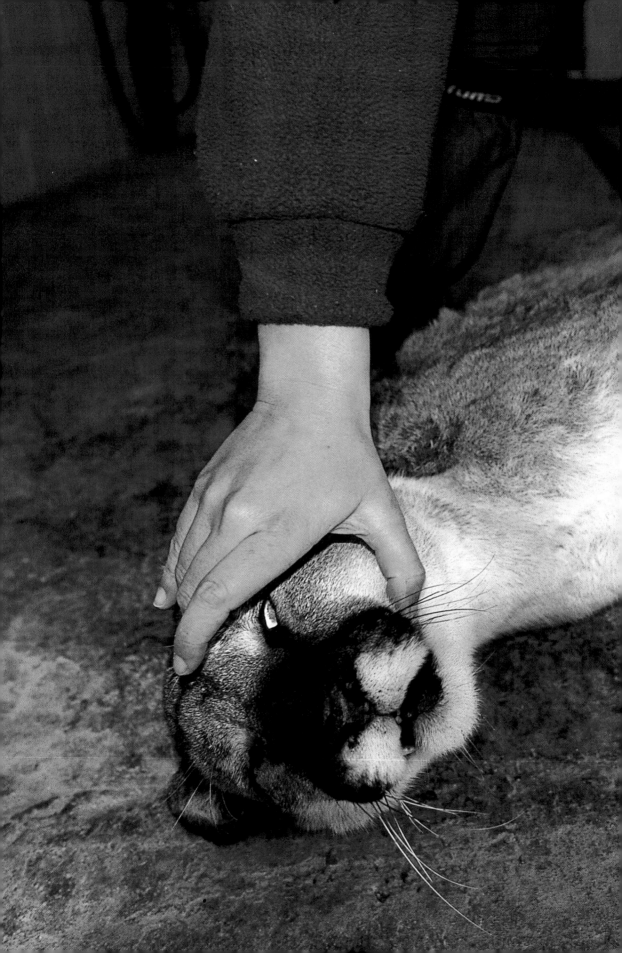

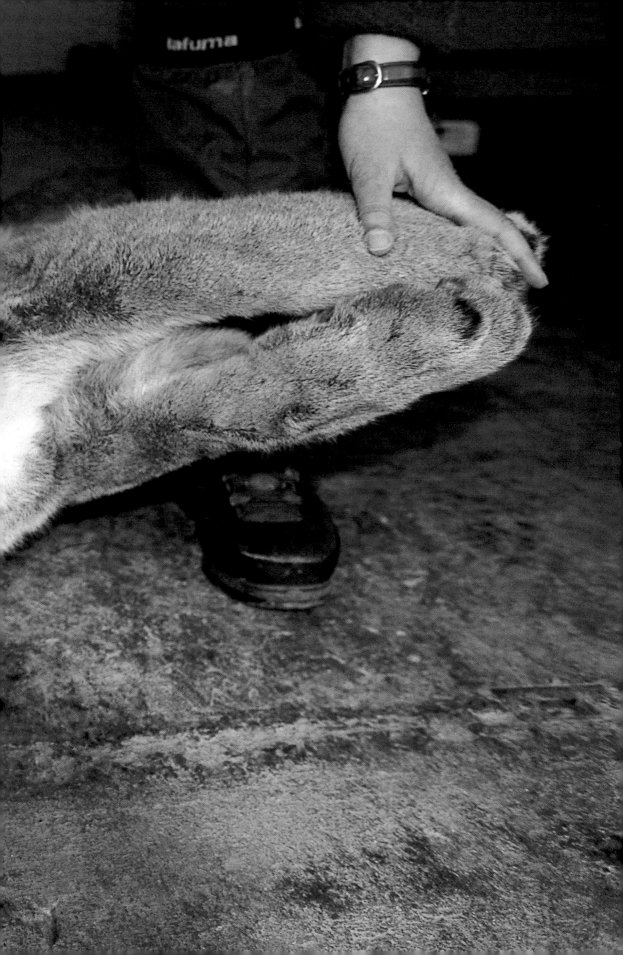

While it was the power of grizzlies that forced this new con-
sciousness, once the leap had been made, it became almost routine to
see other flora and fauna within the same perspective. If elk inside the
reserve's entrance gate were park elk, for example, what were they when
hard winters sent them sifting down out of the mountains right into
the town of Gardiner, Montana? Street elk? Front yard elk? Half a
dozen different national forests surround the park; were those Forest
Service elk? No. Like all the others, they were migratory Greater
Yellowstone elk.

Rather than trumpeter swans that nest in the park and trumpeters
that winter just west in the Henrys Fork of the Snake River and in
Red Rock Lakes National Wildlife Refuge, we have the resident swans
of the entire ecosystem. What used to be park cutthroat trout, or
Bureau of Land Management cutthroat, or the cutthroat that swam
past private riverfront property, all became cutthroat native to the
Greater Yellowstone Ecosystem. It started to seem odd that we had
ever expected free-roaming wildlife to somehow conform to the old
patchwork of public lands and bureaucracies.

As the shortcomings of traditional, segregated reserves became
increasingly apparent from Africa to Australia, we have broadened our
views of nature protection to take in entire landscapes. Thus the
notion of a Greater Yellowstone Ecosystem fits right into the trend of
modern conservation biology. Individual parks and other sanctuaries
still count for a great deal. But to fully function and truly endure, they
have to be part of a working ecosystem.

What does it take, then, to maintain grizzlies in an area indefinitely? Some biologists figure that any large mammal needs a mini-
mum population of around 2,000 to maintain its genetic variation
and potential to bounce back from natural disasters. Okay, but that
many grizz require something on the order of 50,000 square miles,
which amounts to several Greater Yellowstone Ecosystems together—
or perhaps to one ecosystem strategically linked to the next nearest
wildland, which in turn allows travel to another stretch of vital ground.
You can guess where this is leading: straight toward the vision of Y2Y.

During the late 1970s and 1980s, a handful of wolves trotted from
the Canadian Rockies into Montana. Some of the first tracks left by
these international visitors happened to wind past the very cabin I call
home. A pack formed and established a territory along the west side
of Glacier National Park, and my wife and I got used not only to seeing their paw prints but also to hearing their occasional starlight cho-
rus. Outside of the Great Lakes region, these were the first wolves since
the 1920s to successfully make a home in the lower 48 states, where
the species had been classified as endangered since 1974. The Glacier
pack split in two, and it wasn't long before new generations of wolves
began dispersing from this Montana epicenter. Some headed back into

British Columbia and Alberta. Others struck out in the opposite direction and founded additional packs south of the border. Over the years that followed, a few reached the backcountry of central Idaho, and others may have made forays as far south as Yellowstone, though biologists couldn't find proof that any had settled in either place.

The reason I'm able to find wolves in Yellowstone today is that the U.S. Fish & Wildlife Service (USFWS), which oversees endangered species, put these predators here to speed their recovery. During 1995 and 1996, 35 wolves captured in Canada were transplanted into Idaho's 3.4 million-acre Selway–Bitterroot/Frank Church–River of No Return Wilderness complex. Another 31 Canadian wolves were released into Yellowstone. In order to ease the fears of nearby landowners, the reintroduced populations were declared experimental, which allowed managers to relocate or destroy individuals that caused trouble with livestock.

A fair number of ranchers are still plenty upset about having wolves back in the neighborhood. At the same time, some environmentalists think that the USFWS went too far in easing the usual protection for a species at risk. If the arguments sometimes sound shrill, consider how remarkable it is that we are even having them; that after centuries of wolf "control"—the wildlife version of ethnic cleansing—our society saw fit to try wolf restoration. And while the debates grumble on, these predators are again becoming a four-legged fact of life in the West. About 75 to 100 descendants of those natural colonists from Canada now lope across Montana. Another 100 to 150 transplanted wolves and their progeny, along with some natural colonists, range through Idaho; the Greater Yellowstone Ecosystem holds a similar number.

Several years ago, a female wolf radio-collared in Glacier National Park, Montana, showed up 550 miles north in the Canadian Rockies. More recently, a wolf from Yellowstone crossed west into central Idaho, while an Idaho wolf rambled over into Oregon. To newspapers, this has been sensational material. Yet wandering widely to test opportunities in new ranges is business as usual for wolves. It is exactly what they are designed to do with those long legs, effortless trotting gaits, and questing golden eyes.

Another carnivore with an appetite for miles is the wolverine, a 20-to-50-pound member of the weasel family. Researchers have learned that these generally solitary hunter-scavengers might cover 50 miles within 24 hours. Shot, trapped, and poisoned out of the western states, wolverines returned during the latter part of the 20th century from Canada, padding southward along the Rocky Mountains. In other words, they did the same thing wolves did over the same international stretch of backcountry; they just started a couple of decades earlier. Call it a spontaneous Y2Y plan.

On a more official level, the B.C. government announced in the fall of 1997 that it was setting aside nearly 11 million Y2Y acres in the northern end of the province as the new Muskwa-Kechika reserve. Switzerland is smaller; the province of Nova Scotia would be closer in size. In addition to Indians, trappers, guides, and other residents who draw a living from the land, Muskwa-Kechika supports an estimated 800 grizzlies and an equal number of black bears, 900 wolves, 4,000 caribou, 15,000 elk, 22,000 moose, and 1,500 mountain goats. North of Canada's Peace River, the bighorn sheep of the Rockies, *Ovis canadensis*, is replaced by Dall's sheep, *Ovis dalli*. Bighorns are brown with a white rump. Dall's are typically solid white. However, in the southern part of their range, they have a white rump and strikingly dark, gray body instead. As if Muskwa-Kechika didn't already host enough megafauna, add 7,000 of these Dall's sheep in evening dress, better known as Stone's sheep.

Although the reserve is also referred to as the northern Rocky Mountains wilderness, not much more than one-quarter to one-third is to remain actual wilderness, fully protected in its natural state. Development will be allowed in the rest, but under unusually tight rules devised with the participation of local members of First Nations, Canada's coalition of Native American tribes.

Muskwa-Kechika is a showcase of mountains, biological diversity, and people who depend upon the living wealth of an ecosystem. It is also the type of arrangement that can provide for a future together. This is how Y2Y is supposed to work. Conservation strategies are being drawn up for enormous wildland tracts farther north and around Nahanni National Park. On a smaller but equally important scale, biologists are tweaking computer models of the Yellowstone ecosystem, searching for the best blend of available habitat, open space, and human activities that could serve as a bridge leading northward from this grandfather of national parks.

I KEEP COMING BACK to grizzlies and wolves because big carnivores and our fascination with them have driven so much of the landscape-level approach to conservation. But while prowling around the core of the Rockies, I also met the next tier of predators that animate Y2Y, notably lynx, river otters, fishers, bull trout, and eagles. I spent equally wild times in the company of harlequin ducks, which court and rear young along the high country's whitewater rivers; with the bumptious grey birds called ouzels, or dippers, that nest behind waterfalls and stroll underwater to feed; and with blue grouse, which migrate up-slope in winter to forage on subalpine conifers when practically everything else is headed downhill toward warmer elevations.

Everything, that is, except the race known as mountain caribou. They climb the mountain shoulders to where the snow lies 10 to 20 feet deep or more. I trudge behind them on snowshoes in northern Idaho until I am almost on the skyline. When I finally catch up, I understand. Their own version of snowshoes—huge hoofs—let them use the ever-mounting snowpack to reach golden-green lichens that hang in profusion from high tree branches. Again, I think: Here I am many hundreds of miles from Nahanni Park, in a different nation, yet still among row after row of mountains, still among caribou, and, yes, there are a few wolves around too.

I know animals aren't the only reason I keep migrating deeper into the Rockies myself, but I'm not sure I can describe what the other reasons are. Or if they are even reasons. Some have more in common with prayer. Maybe a white man's vision quest is more like it; the vistas up there are pure rocket fuel for the spirit. Then again, a lot of the attraction has to do with the folks I meet on the way up and down: the loggers, miners, ranchers, and their families who inhabit the current outposts of civilization. And the native people who have been there all along. Their traditional knowledge still braids the strands of human culture into the web of life on all sides. Can some of the ancient ways circle round to guide us into the future, from Yellowstone to the Yukon?

You never know what's on the other side of the mountain until you see for yourself. If you wander north of Whitehorse in the Yukon, you might stumble upon rock formed by volcanic activity in Yellowstone millions of years earlier, for as pressure from the Pacific seafloor squeezed the Rockies upward, parts of the crust slid north along a major fault line. Hot springs scattered throughout the region today are further testimony to the grinding, squeezing, molten forces at work below many a white peak with blue glaciers.

Of all the beauty and marvels that Y2Y holds, though, the ones that are alive seem to me the best of all. West of Jasper National Park, Mount Robson soars almost two miles up from a valley where grizzlies snag migrating Pacific salmon on the mossy, fern-strewn stream banks of an interior rain forest hundreds of miles from the sea. Just across the Continental Divide from my Montana home, Blackfeet Indians recently released swift foxes from Canada onto their reservation in an attempt to restore this threatened species. From edge to edge, the biological riches of the region are a global treasure.

With its unsurpassed collection of reserves and the potential for ensuring habitat linkages and movement corridors between them, Y2Y is fundamentally about the vitality of nature and our connection to it over centuries to come. I know of no better hope for strengthening the backbone of the continent, no surer way to safeguard the Rockies' extraordinary wildlife communities along with the processes that sustain them—and ultimately sustain us, in body and soul. ◆

FOLLOWING PAGES:
RAM PLATEAU, NORTHWEST TERRITORIES
Pure white Dall's sheep race along the aptly named Ram Plateau, a remote and immense limestone karstland north of Nahanni National Park Reserve in the Northwest Territories. Farther south along the Rockies, they are replaced by Stone's sheep, which have darker coats. A third type of mountain sheep—bighorns—take over south of Canada's Peace River.

THE
SOUTHERN
APPROACH

YELLOWSTONE NATIONAL PARK
◆ FRANK CHURCH-RIVER OF NO RETURN
WILDERNESS ◆ GOSPEL HUMP WILDERNESS
◆ SELWAY-BITTERROOT WILDERNESS
◆ SHOSHONE NATIONAL FOREST ◆ GRAND
TETON NATIONAL PARK ◆ NATIONAL ELK
REFUGE ◆ BRIDGER-TETON NATIONAL
FOREST ◆ SCAPEGOAT/BOB MARSHALL/
GREAT BEAR WILDERNESS ◆ FREEZOUT LAKE
WILDLIFE MANAGEMENT AREA
◆ GLACIER NATIONAL PARK

PREVIOUS PAGES:
LAMAR RIVER
Poised for adventure,
river otters by the edge
of this Yellowstone
stream might be ready
for a play wrestling
match, a slide down
a steep snowbank,
or a dash through icy
waters to hunt trout.
While the area's big
animals—megafauna,
to biologists—tend
to capture the public's
attention, creatures
of every size contribute
to the balance of an
ecosystem. And some,
like this pair, add
more than their share
of sparkle.

BEGINNING at Y2Y's southwestern edge, the already high deserts of eastern Oregon and southern Idaho merge into higher slopes that lift and cool passing air masses, making them more generous with rain. Here, sagebrush and other drought-tolerant shrubs that rule the Great Basin give way to juniper, then to phalanxes of ponderosa and lodgepole pines. Deeper and still higher into the Rockies, the forests steadily thicken. Groves of western red cedar, a sure indicator of abundant moisture, appear. Valleys thrum with the tumbling headwaters of the Clearwater, Lochsa, Selway, and Lemhi rivers and the Snake River's major tributary, the Salmon.

With miles of rapids detonating between canyon walls of volcanic rock, the Salmon proved such a barrier to navigation that early white travelers labeled it the River of No Return. Of course, the namesake fish surged through every year, no more deterred by its turbulence than the falcons that nest along the river's cliffs are by heights. Then a succession of dams built across the Columbia and Snake turned one Rocky Mountain waterway after another into a true river of no return for these marathon swimmers. Steelhead, recently reclassified as a form of salmon, still thrash upstream among Idaho's peaks. But by the 1990s, the only other evidence of Pacific salmon that once arrived by the tens of thousands was an endangered handful of sockeye still struggling to Redfish Lake in the Sawtooth Mountains.

A positive change on the wildlife front came in 1980, when the rugged backcountry of the Salmon was officially protected as the Frank Church-River of No Return Wilderness. This reserve's northern border adjoins the Gospel Hump Wilderness and the Selway-Bitterroot Wilderness, which spills into Montana. In all, the three reserves encompass 5.6 million pristine acres; they are surrounded by more than 15 million acres of fairly remote, intact, and mostly public lands, such as national forests. Combine all of these, and you have what conservation biologists call the Salmon-Selway ecosystem. Similar in size to the Greater Yellowstone Ecosystem, the Salmon-Selway is one of the principal wildland strongholds remaining in the southern Y2Y.

Even today, hiking across the wilderness portion of the Bitterroot Range can be reminiscent of the days when Lewis and Clark scouted for a way through these heights. Eagles nest on the same crags, and freshly tracked game trails still lead across the passes. High-elevation stands of subalpine fir and Engelmann spruce continue to flourish unbroken by chainsaws or bulldozer blades. The same tree I lean against today may have sheltered a Shoshone, Salish, or Nez Perce Indian traveler from the era before contact. The longer I linger here, the less important my watch becomes. Hours and days take on a whole different meaning when you can no longer tell which century you are in.

It was along the eastern slope of the Bitterroots, in the Bass Creek watershed, that I saw my first mountain goat emerge from a blizzard, part flesh-and-blood, part perfect snow sculpture. Almost three decades later, I have returned to the exact spot—and found a nanny and her kid on the rock ledges above. But it is April now, and these white goats have their noses in emerald-green shoots up on the sun-facing cliffs. Downstream, I pass from official wilderness to the portion of the national forest managed for a variety of uses. The canyon constricts, squirting me into the wide, open, and even more rapidly greening Bitterroot Valley. A short distance away, the gentle slopes are cleared and fenced and lowed over by cattle, a cross of Hereford and Angus, many only a few days old. It is calving time on the Ruffatto ranch.

Tom Ruffatto, part of the third generation to run this livestock outfit, tells me, "Grandpa Feronato left the Italian army to come to the U.S. before World War I. He was headed for Cheyenne, Wyoming. The thing is, Cheyenne is pronounced Cayana in Italian, and that name was never announced on the train. Grandpa ended up back in Denver. Then he got a free ride to Montana by signing on to work in the sugar beet fields. Eventually, he came here and ended up getting this land from a realtor in the '30s just for putting up fencing and paying the taxes."

Today, you might still swap field labor for a train ticket, but you'd need saddlebags of money to get any acreage in the scenic Bitterroot Valley, rapidly filling with trophy homes, ranchettes, and bedroom communities for nearby Missoula. As I drive with Ruffatto to the upper part of his property, I can see the town of Stevensville stretching out along the valley floor beyond the Bitterroot River and Highway 93. On our side the pastures are stippled with elk, which rely upon valley

ranchlands for winter and early spring range. Ruffatto's is one of the few large tracts that remains undivided; that's why the animals are here.

A bull elk still carrying antlers lifts its head as we admire its 800-pound, chocolate-and-silver form. Ruffatto points to some serviceberry brush and says quietly, "Something smaller moving this way. A deer, most likely. We get a lot of them wintering down here too." But the animal that emerges is shorter than a deer. It is a male wolf.

The elk stands its ground as the newcomer pads toward him and then continues past, giving us a sidelong glance. For a guy with baby beef lying around his warming meadows like hors d'oeuvres on a platter, Tom Ruffatto seems pretty relaxed. He is no fan of predators, having grown up hearing his grandfather's tales of how wolves tore into sheep herds before the valley's last pack was snuffed out in the 1920s. But like the elk, this cowboy is content for now to just watch the wolf trot slowly uphill and into the woods.

"A pair of wolves showed up two falls ago," Ruffatto recalls. "They hung around over winter with the elk. Come spring, they left with the elk back into the mountains. The biologists had radios on the wolves, so they know they denned way up around Lolo Pass and had five pups. Later the same spring, I was chasing some cows when I saw what I thought were coyotes in the distance. Closer up, I could see they were grown wolves—different ones, because neither was wearing a collar."

At first, it was assumed that the wolves were descended from those reintroduced to the central Idaho wilderness in 1995 and 1996. Since Idaho's local politicians refused to let the state game department bring back wolves, the Nez Perce tribe had assumed responsibility for the endangered species in that state, working in cooperation with the U.S. Fish and Wildlife Service (USFWS). The animals seemed to be surviving and reproducing at a healthy rate. Still, it was too early to say when, or even if, the experimental population would become sufficiently large for officials to declare wolf recovery a success.

One of the two new visitors to Ruffatto's place got caught in a coyote trap set by a recreational trapper. Biologists showed up, ready to relocate the pair if asked. While the trapped male howled and the female answered from the mountainside, Ruffatto knew he had a decision to make. He talked things over with his neighbor, Ed Cummings.

"We kind of felt that if we pressed to get rid of the pair, we might never know whether we had stopped wolves from making a comeback," Ruffatto says as he gooses his four-wheel-drive rig through a soggy spot. "We thought: Let's give 'em a chance, see how things play out."

Biologists then radio-collared the trapped male and promised that if problems with livestock developed, agents would hustle out to remove the cause. Compensation for any proven losses from wolves would be paid by Defenders of Wildlife, a conservation group that had set up a fund for that purpose. "The wolves killed a stray dog," Ruffatto continues, "and they dug up the body of a cow I'd buried. But we haven't had a lick of trouble with our livestock that I know of."

Part of the reason may lie in a metal box he shows me by a cottonwood-lined draw full of willow brush, the main natural path through the meadows for any predator seeking concealment. The box houses a radio receiver that, upon sensing the normal signal from the male wolf's collar within 300 to 500 yards, trips a switch to activate a pair of prototype wolf-repellers. Set high in a tree on either side of the gully, each combines a car alarm with a flashing strobe light.

A federal biologist cobbled together the gadgetry, but the idea for an aversion device that would respond to an animal's radio collar came from Ed Cummings, who I learn may have lost at least one calf to wolves before the capture. I've heard stockmen cuss away for hours on end about wolves, promising to give any they see the old triple-S treatment: Shoot, Shovel, and Shut-up. Why did Cummings bother to look for a brand-new solution? I drive straight over to his ranch to ask.

"First, we ranchers take pride in helping things live," replies Cummings, a former pro football player who gripped my hand in his large paw and invited me in to share a late dinner. "It seems a shame to have to be killing instead. Second, four days before the wolf was trapped, I watched the pair just coming over a rise, and it was one of the most beautiful sights I had ever seen. And third, I thought maybe other people ought to be able to see something like that. Or at least take a hike and have the hope of seeing something like that."

Wolves within ranch country have gone months or even years without touching tame meat—far longer than many predicted was possible. But then comes a hard winter that halves the abundance of natural prey, or a denning season when a pack is struggling to feed a big litter of growing pups. Nothing guarantees that the next sunrise won't reveal fresh livestock blood seeping into the pasture.

Weeks later, I am told that the collared male and his mate did not follow the elk back into the mountains but denned in the foothills scarcely a mile from Ruffatto's place. There the female gave birth to eight pups. After two of another neighbor's calves disappeared, officials found the carcass of a third and confirmed that wolves had caused its death. As promised, they removed the pack to holding pens. From ear tags, they discovered that the adult female had come 140 miles south from the Murphy Lake pack, part of the population naturally recolonizing Montana from Canada. The adult male suffered an injured foot during capture, and when a biologist later tried to examine it, a restraining noose accidentally locked, choking the animal to death. Then three of the pups succumbed to parvovirus, probably contracted from dogs.

While the novel blend of technology and tolerance I witnessed along Bass Creek did not lead to a storybook ending, neither can it be counted a failure. Just a generation ago, wolf management in this part of the country simply meant making sure there weren't any. Live ones were considered an oversight. Yes, several died this time, too, but the mother and five pups survived and were released on the edge of Montana's Bob Marshall Wilderness during the winter, in the hope that they will establish a territory farther from temptation. However it plays out, their saga will continue to make newspaper headlines.

Attitudes toward predators are clearly changing in the new West. A recent USFWS proposal proves the point by daring to suggest the re-establishment of grizzly bears. Only two major populations of grizzlies remain in the lower 48 states, one inhabiting the greater Yellowstone, one in the Glacier Park area ecosystem. USFWS experts think this threatened species' chances for recovery would improve significantly if a third major group could be added. How? By putting grizzlies back into the huge Salmon-Selway ecosystem.

On average, the total damage to livestock by the 350 to 450 wolves now in the southern Y2Y comes to about $30,000 annually. So, though the losses can still hurt sharply for any one family, we are basically talking about the cost of a new car over a tri-state region. Depredations by the 700 to 1,000 grizzlies living south of Canada add up to less than half that amount. The big difference is that a single grizzly in a rotten mood can cost you an arm and a leg—literally. Never mind how rarely that happens. If statistics outweighed primal fears, we wouldn't keep horses or dogs. They kill or maim more Westerners every year than *horribilis* has in all the years since anyone started keeping count.

At a cafe along Highway 93, two women take time from busy ranch workdays to meet with me and explain the position of a local group called Concerned About Grizzlies. Typically, the restaurant decor features portraits of wolves, bighorn sheep, and other majestic wildlife. One print, entitled "High and Mighty," portrays an eagle and grizzly bear duo. The next wall holds a signed poster of an archer with a humongous Kodiak bear dead at his feet. Folks around here obviously admire big bruins in one form or another.

"Our number one concern is safety," Shirley Bugli informs me. "Defenders of Wildlife might compensate for livestock losses, yes. But who can put a value on the life of a child? Who will be accountable? Our second main objection is the cost of the reintroduction and the bureaucracy that will come with it."

"We don't hate bears, and we don't love 'em," adds Rosemarie Neuman, the endangered species chairperson for WIFE—Women Involved in Farm Economics. "We say just don't put any in here. Keep them where they are. Leave things alone. If we have grizzlies, it's going to shut us down. Are we supposed to pack up and leave? The federal government is out of hand. They use environmental issues as a method of control." Before departing, the women hand me newsletters and clippings to the effect that grizzly recovery is merely a ploy by political schemers whose real agenda is globalization. Their plan apparently involves declaring parks and wilderness areas World Heritage Sites or International Biosphere Reserves sanctioned by the United Nations—a practice that could herald a takeover of American soil, warns a Bitterroot Valley member of the Montana legislature. Although I can't follow all the reasoning, I gain a new respect for the depth of people's concern about outside forces affecting their way of life.

REMARKABLY, Bitterroot Valley residents are about equally divided over the proposal to have grizzlies move in next door. Another surprise has been the coalition formed by representatives from pro-wildlife organizations and the timber industry, groups usually busy quarreling. Their plan, called the Citizens' Management Alternative, favors grizz reintroduction (albeit in a much smaller area than that recommended by wildlife scientists) and it fosters an unprecedented level of local involvement in the recovery process as the bears spread outward from the wilderness core. This compromise speaks to the fact that many Westerners don't object to wildlife—even occasionally dangerous species—so much as to regulations that they feel hamper local economies and infringe upon individual rights.

The Bitterroot Valley is so broad and the mountains so imposing that calling the place a microcosm doesn't seem quite right. Nevertheless, it does encapsulate a whole suite of issues common to the Y2Y region from the southern terrain well into Canada. (Geologically, the valley represents the southern end of a Y2Y feature known as the Rocky Mountain Trench, a continuous string of troughs that runs along the western side of the great divide for more than a thousand miles.) What used to be the boondocks have more recently become busy test sites for the priorities of two nations that share strong pioneer heritages and a rapidly shrinking, ever more valuable supply of genuine frontiers. For that matter, the question of how to manage growth and development has surged to the fore in almost every community on the continent.

Before carnivore comebacks became the hot topic, Bitterrooters were arguing over timber on public lands. Years of heavy logging and roadbuilding took a toll on watersheds, fisheries, and wildlife populations. It also made merchantable trees harder to find and more expensive. When agencies reduced allowable harvests to more sustainable levels, local sawmills had little choice but to begin laying off workers. Technological advances within the industry made more jobs obsolete. Then, as demands to better protect other woodland resources pared the timber volume further, one mill after another closed.

While loggers went bust, real estate boomed. Rocky Mountain

recreation and scenery had been bid up into prized commodities. Look around, podner, they ain't making any more of this stuff. The valley comes with the kind of views that practically close sales by themselves. Yet for many urban refugees, the overriding attraction was a stable, secure, rural environment in which to raise families or retire. While ads touted Montana as the last, best place, Ravalli County, which encompasses most of the Bitterroot Valley, became one of the fastest-growing areas in the region. Subdivisions sprawled unchecked. Winter ranges and other vital wildlife habitats shrank. Traffic congestion spread like plaque along the two-lane road artery, where the bumper stickers read Pray For Me, I Drive Highway 93. With new waves of settlers eroding the very qualities they were seeking, land-use planning became another loud controversy.

Even today, Ravalli County has no comprehensive zoning rules or strategy for growth. That, say property rights activists, is a Western tradition we ought to keep. Some object to the very word planning. Other home owners think insisting that we still have room for unrestrained development is like saying: fire away, boys, there's no end to these buffalo herds. Whatever residents ultimately decide will affect the other Bitterroot issues under debate. Like bears.

REINTRODUCING grizzlies into the Salmon-Selway ecosystem would put them about 140 miles from Yellowstone and within 40 miles of a small, dwindling pocket of great bears in the Cabinet-Yaak country of northwestern Montana. The value of the reintroduction will diminish if these groups remain isolated from one another. Conversely, to the extent that they make contact and mingle genes, the long-term future of each population and the species as a whole would brighten. Experts calculate that an exchange of just one or two males per grizzly generation is enough to prevent inbreeding. But how to connect them? Much of the land between the bear populations is private. How much will be developed? How heavily? What kind of passageways can be secured for bears—as well as for wolves, wolverines, and other carnivores that require large, joined blocks of habitat to survive? For herbivores? For native vegetation?

At rush hour, portions of Highway 93 carry as many as 1,500 vehicles per hour, or 25 every minute. An anticipated expansion to four and five lanes will make driving faster and presumably safer for humans. But without a redesign to include underpasses or overpasses in the animals' prime travel routes, the roadkill total of everything from bobcats to elk is bound to, well, bloat. Black bears get creamed each year trying to cross the two-lane, along with about 500 deer. Hard-won improvements in forest management won't help fisheries where too many new fertilized lawns and septic systems drain into creeks. And the meadows blazing with wildflowers in the backcountry won't maintain elk herds if their winter range in the valley turns into scenic homesites.

The work of conserving nature can be tremendously complex and intimidating. But like the processes of natural selection, adaptation, and renewal—like life itself—it is a profound expression of optimism. If you fret that the situation for wildlife gets worse every year, look again at those elk on the Bitterroot's slopes—and count back 100 years, to when this species was wiped out across most of North America. Its history through the last century represents a stunning conservation success, one of many that heighten our present-day experience of the outdoors. The challenge is to keep the triumphs aglow.

A century ago, the continent's last real bastion for elk was at the southeastern end of Y2Y, in the ecosystem focused around Yellowstone Park, protected from hunting since 1872. Roughly 25,000 of the animals wintered south of the park in a spectacular valley between the Teton and Gros Ventre Ranges. Although its average elevation exceeds 6,000 feet, this peak-sheltered bottomland collects relatively little snow. Trappers used to rendezvous here alongside the elk, bison, and deer. The spot was named for David Jackson, partner of one of the better known mountain men, William Sublette.

The first homesteaders didn't arrive until 1884, making Jackson Hole among the last valleys in the West to be settled. All too soon, the elk were being commercially hunted for meat and their rounded canine teeth, popular as jewelry. As more of the valley was parcelled into ranch pastures, hooved wildlife came to be viewed as competitors for forage. Much of the annual grass supply was cut and hauled off as hay. When winter turned extra tough and starving elk came around the storage cribs for a bite, stockmen shot them by the droves.

What good was Yellowstone as an elk sanctuary if the traditional winter range outside the park was turning lethal? Congress responded in 1912 by establishing the National Elk Refuge in the heart of Jackson Hole. The original reserve was small. In 1927, the Izaak Walton League helped expand it through the purchase of ranchland. Two years later, the scenic high country between the refuge and Yellowstone Park became Grand Teton National Park. Local ranchers Si Ferrin and Pierce Cunningham had already begun a drive to set aside the valley "for the education and enjoyment of the Nation as a whole." Their efforts bore fruit when much of the bottomland was declared a national monument that was later added to Grand Teton. Meanwhile, the National Elk Refuge expanded toward its current total of 24,700 acres directly adjoining the southern boundary of 310,520-acre Grand Teton.

Here was an early example of linkage at the landscape level, the concept behind today's Y2Y Conservation Initiative. In any one decade, protecting wildlands may seem impractical or excessive, a hindrance to the way business is done. Yet with the *Continued on page 56*

THE SOUTHERN APPROACH
MAJOR ISSUES

Managing the numbers: Naturally selective, wolves have shaped wild ungulate species through generations of trial-by-chase. Yet for more than half a century, North America's most widespread and efficient predators were conspicuously absent from the world's first national park. During that era, when some biologists and even some ranchers spoke of Yellowstone's big, bad animals, they meant elk, which proliferated and altered park range through heavy grazing and trampling. But today the wolves are back—for now.

THE SOUTHERN APPROACH

WILLIAM CAMPBELL

Myth vs. reality: A popular symbol of things wild and free, the wolf finds today's American West a cold, hard ground. The 300-plus wolves now in the early stages of recovery are heavily managed to minimize conflicts with local people, many of whom view them as symbols of unwanted federal intervention. Pack members that trouble livestock face reloca-tion or death. Bison that roam outside Yellowstone face the same fate. In the winter of 1996-97, 1,100 out of a total park population of 3,500 bison were shot for that transgression, sparking protests from Indian tribes (right). Ranchers fear the shaggy grazers will contaminate cattle with brucellosis, a disease that can induce abortion, although evidence of transmission from wild herds is scant.

Jokingly referred to as slow elk, cattle share Red Rock Lakes National Wildlife Refuge in the Centennial Valley west of Yellowstone (left) with true elk—whose antlers adorn many a barn (above). The issue of livestock grazing on public lands puts resource officials on the horns of a dilemma. Critics say heavy use by domestic herds degrades soils, water quality, and forage available for wildlife while inviting conflicts with resident predators. But supporters point to significant improvements in management over the years.

Home on whose range? The 15- to 20-million-acre Greater Yellowstone Ecosystem harbors North America's largest concentration of elk—currently around 125,000 animals, including this band feasting on spring green-up in Wyoming's Sunlight Basin (opposite). They rove across a mix of lands that include private pastures and Shoshone National Forest. Mule deer (above) also jump back and forth between private, state, and federal real estate. The future of both species hinges upon closer cooperation between the varied land managers involved.

THE SOUTHERN APPROACH

Off on a jaunt in Shoshone National Forest—just past Yellowstone's border—this mother grizz and two cubs delight human passersby, perhaps convincing them that wildlife here is intact and abundant. The real story, however, is that grizzlies in Greater Yellowstone fell to an all-time low of 150 to 300 individuals during the 1970s. Though they now appear to be rebounding, the number of people on private lands surrounding the park continues to outpace that recovery. The area's human population is expected to double again within the next few decades, raising the specter of increased human-bruin interactions and a rise in "problem bears."

passage of time, society almost always finds itself enormously grateful, having come to regard those same places as priceless national treasures.

Elk from Yellowstone Park and the National Elk Refuge have been used to restock 25 states and two Canadian provinces. Back home in the Greater Yellowstone Ecosystem, the animals have increased to 125,000, the largest concentration of their kind in North America. Outings in the wildlife refuge, combined with trips to Grand Teton Park and recreation centers such as ski resorts, support a prospering tourist industry. Horse-drawn sleighs alone carry nearly 30,000 elk-viewers through the refuge each winter. As another gauge of what people think sharing such country is worth, private land in and around the town of Jackson, which abuts the southwestern corner of the National Elk Refuge, now goes for upward of a million dollars per acre.

"I think we had half the town coming out every day this spring," Bruce Smith, the refuge's chief biologist, tells me on a sunny afternoon in mid-May. "A mother cougar raised three kittens right there, more or less in plain view." He is pointing at shallow caves near the base of Miller Butte, 200 feet from the road and less than a mile from the edge of Jackson. "We were seeing a trio of wolves on the refuge most of the winter," Smith continues, "and the Soda Butte pack made at least three trips here from Yellowstone. Right now, there's yet another pack denning in Grand Teton Park." Like their counterparts in the Bitterroot Valley, these wolves are something new to the modern panorama.

No matter where Smith directs my attention—to bighorn sheep that have spread to the butte from nearby mountains, to nesting trumpeter swans, to sandhill cranes, to creeks harboring cutthroat trout—my gaze keeps going off to scale the Tetons. The range, which includes a dozen peaks above 12,000 feet, vacuums up sight. The next day, while gaping at that skyline, I help Smith sample the condition of forage in the park. Band after band of elk migrating north from the refuge intersect our hiking route through copses of aspen and pines floored with yellowbells. Smith keeps an eye out for any lone female reluctant to leave as we draw near—a sign that she may have a new baby stashed nearby in the sagebrush or grass.

As he has the previous two springs, Smith will capture about 50 elk calves, place radio transmitters on them, then follow the signals to discover the animals' fate. Almost 30 percent die within five to six weeks of birth, mostly from predation. Although the figure is not unusual for wild ungulates, it has doubled from the 1980s. Black bears are the principal predators of elk calves here, followed by coyotes. Smith thinks the doubling of calf mortality partly reflects an increasing cougar population, along with the growing presence of grizzlies.

Not long ago, Greg Holm, presently working for the Wyoming Game and Fish Department, set out bait stations to trap and collar bears in Grand Teton Park and the adjoining Bridger-Teton National

Forest. He expected black bears, but never thought he would catch 24 within his modest-size study area. And he was astounded when 18 different grizzlies wound up in his traps as well. Grizz had been considered a rarity south of Yellowstone Park for a quarter of a century or more. The fact that they are colonizing this part of the ecosystem suggests that Yellowstone's once imperiled, long controversial, always hard-to-count grizzly population is bouncing back from its low point.

The addition of grizzlies and wolves to elk country might not strike everyone as wonderful news. Yet elk evolved and thrived under precisely such pressures. Not long after steps were taken to safeguard herds in the Yellowstone ecosystem from excessive human hunting, managers began to worry about overcrowding, and resorted to drastic control hunts. Culling operations ended in 1967, and the elk biomass has since nearly doubled. This explains why the Yellowstone wolf restoration is loping along well ahead of schedule. Superabundant elk also appear to be a major factor driving the rebound of grizzlies.

I N SHORT, the balance is swinging back toward nature's definition of normal. Not that it is likely to get there anytime soon. Despite having been enlarged over the years, the National Elk Refuge takes in only a fragment of the prime bottomland meadows that herds relied upon before Jackson Hole was settled. To accommodate the elk that begin piling in with the first snows, workers provide extra food in the form of alfalfa pellets. This feedlot setting makes an ideal hunting ground for invisible enemies—microbes that jump from one warm body to the next via runny noses, saliva, and droppings.

More than one-third of the elk and three-quarters of the bison on the refuge test positive for exposure to the bacterium *Brucella abortis*. An active infection, known as brucellosis, can cause females to abort developing fetuses. Ranchers and livestock regulators are jittery about the disease spreading to cattle. Some are calling for an end to artificial feeding of elk, coupled with a reduction in their numbers. Others want federal officials to somehow round up and immunize free-roaming ungulate herds, though a surefire vaccine has yet to be developed.

Bison often leave Yellowstone in search of food, especially during heavy snow years. Over the hard winter of 1996-97, almost 1,100—one of every three in the park—were slaughtered to protect domestic stock. Nearly 100 more were killed the next winter, despite loud objections from the public, particularly Native Americans, who offered to transfer the wandering bison to reservations.

Ironically, it is almost certain that the elk and bison contracted brucellosis from livestock rather than vice versa. Moreover, actual cases of transmission from wildlife to livestock are so rare and poorly documented that critics wonder how much of the problem is bureaucratic panic and cow country politics feeding off one another. A better understanding of *Brucella* in its wild hosts is sorely needed, which is why I'm riding horseback beside veterinarian John Murnane in the northern valley of Yellowstone Park. I'm sunbaked and wind-chafed and tall in the saddle, easy on the reins but a hard man to turn aside. I ain't no cowboy, pilgrim, I'm a buffaloboy, hazing a fair-size bunch of bison along an open bench high above the Lamar River under the prettiest mountain sky May ever made.

The lead bison cow breaks into a trot, and all at once the herd is galloping downhill, headed for a copse of Douglas fir by the edge of a creek, just as we hoped. Hiding there are Jack Rhyan, a disease investigator from the National Wildlife Research Center, and Keith Aune, supervisor of the Montana Department of Fish, Wildlife and Parks Wildlife Research Laboratory. Murnane and I scramble to keep the stampeders from reversing course. Below, Aune takes a shot with a dart filled with a potent immobilizing compound. By the time I dismount at the ambush spot, a pregnant cow bison is settling onto her knees on the far bank of the creek, and the melt-swollen water is full of plunging humans and pitching horses on their way to her side.

While Murnane carefully monitors the drugged female's condition and administers bottled oxygen to supplement her breathing, Rhyan and Aune collect blood, secretions from every moist orifice possible, and milk. "Almost half the females we test have antibodies that indicate exposure to *Brucella*," Rhyan says, "but it's a sneaky disease. It can hide in just one organ and stay there quietly for a long time. On females, we use vaginal implant radios designed to drop out at birth so we can locate the site and tell whether the calf was aborted or not. It sure looks like some bison calves were."

Later, I turn my horse over to someone else and walk the miles back to our starting point past blossoming larkspur and aspen leaves that have unfurled noticeably since morning. Alone with my thoughts, I ask a passing raven whether every wild animal in the country is going to wind up with a radio beeping somewhere on its body. Perhaps this is only a symptom of our era, and once we have enough data, we can start figuring out how to leave the creatures alone. The raven circles to say Quork! Quork! Tok! and veers away north.

I look beyond the bird and recognize a distant hillside, where I watched a wolf den earlier in the month. The pups were two weeks old at the time and had just begun to explore outside the den, dug beneath a gigantic boulder. A baby romped and bumbled onto the side of a black wolf, one of several grown-ups snoozing by the den mouth. When the pup was done nibbling its relative's ear and tried to leave, the black wolf casually pinned down its tail with a paw. Four little legs spun in the dirt, making absolutely no progress at all, until the adult gave the little wolf a nuzzle and let it pop free. Beside me, Doug Smith, who heads the park wolf research team, commented, "Ah, yes, there they are—the beasts of waste and desolation."

THOSE MEMORIES evaporate along with my calm as I realize that I have come upon a bachelor band of very stout bull bison resting on the grass. Yessir, a buffaloboy afoot is a far more humble fellow than the mounted version. Bison, after all, have bashed a few Yellowstone visitors as thoroughly as grizzlies have. But these bachelors look to be in an easygoing mood. They merely stand up, still chewing cuds, while I detour toward some big climbable boulders the glaciers left on the bench thousands of years ago.

That evening, I meet Wade Peck, a rancher in the Paradise Valley just north of the park, between the Gallatin and Absaroka mountain ranges. "You know how the cow business is these days," he begins. "You buy retail, sell wholesale, and pay the freight both ways. You can't control the weather or the markets or your neighbors, and our neighbors are the park animals and park bureaucracy. We get wintering bison, elk, and bighorn sheep and plenty of sightings of bears and wolves. I'm not real upset by the actual conflicts with wildlife. I just don't need the headaches, the politics, or the risk that I can't sell cattle because buyers are worried about brucellosis."

In fact, Peck is phasing out of beef and now works for an electronics company. But when we speak, he and a partner still run 500 cow-calf pairs. All the other stockmen in this area from which so many bison have been removed own barely 150 head of cattle among them. One way to reduce exposure to disease is to feed the cattle on more distant pastures through the winter, when wildlife comes seeking native forage. To make more wildlife range available during that critical season, the privately funded Rocky Mountain Elk Foundation is working with the Forest Service to acquire portions of a large ranch on the park border—a ranch where Peck once worked.

Roughly 40 miles north, the Gallatin Mountains overlook the growing city of Bozeman, Montana. There, I make my way to the office of Lance Craighead, who wants to know where wildlife can travel once they leave the Greater Yellowstone Ecosystem entirely. Establishing or reconstructing long distance connections through habitat corridors is one of the most important and difficult tasks in conservation biology. For guidance, Craighead looks to the heavens, criss-crossed by orbiting satellites.

His walls are filled with striking maps of landforms based on remote sensing data from space. On his desktops, humming computers download the latest digital details about southern Y2Y terrain. Lance is the son of Frank Craighead, who, with his brother John, developed the technique of tracking wildlife with radio collars and handheld antennas. The brothers went on to help devise collars whose signals could be monitored by satellite. They were also among the first to use satellite imagery to analyze wildlife habitats. Their special interest was grizzly bears. So is Lance's.

"When Dad and John started, it took two to four weeks at a computer with the help of a technician to put together a map," Lance remembers. "The software I use can assemble a much more refined picture of the terrain, vegetation, and key foods in one or two hours. What I'm trying to do is view the landscape through the needs of native creatures. The grizzly is our umbrella species, because the area it requires covers the home ranges of so many other kinds of wildlife. But in defining critical habitat, we sometimes go less on what the bears prefer than on where people aren't. We have to pick out places where human impacts are minimal. Roads are a big factor. Grizzlies avoid them. The few that don't run a higher risk of getting shot."

He shows me a map revealing a mostly roadless corridor northward from the Gallatin and Bridger Ranges toward the southern end of the Scapegoat/Bob Marshall/Great Bear wilderness complex, connected in turn to Glacier Park. A second backcountry avenue leads westward from Yellowstone through the Centennial Valley area toward the Bitterroot Range. Less obvious routes spiderweb across a mixture of wild settings and rural countrysides.

The map is a blueprint of possibilities. It also highlights the weakest links in the wildland chain, showing agencies where extra protection might be called for on the public land portions. Where a potential travelway includes private property, non-government organizations can try to set up conservation easements, offering owners substantial tax breaks or outright payments if they agree to limit certain kinds of development such as subdivision. Such win-win arrangements are an increasingly popular tool for land-use planning from coast to coast.

What intrigues me is the blending of hi-tech data beamed from spacecraft with the old, untamable, earthen muscle and marrow of the great bear. While Craighead models grizzly bear corridors in the southern Y2Y region, an atlas produced by Canadian contributors to the Y2Y Conservation Initiative extends the computer portrait of grizzly bear habitat northward into Yukon Territory. We primates are highly visual animals, but our eyes are only a few feet off the ground. The new maps allow us to behold the world from a perspective beyond that of any eagle, mountaineer, or airplane pilot. For the first time, we can visualize how we and wildlife fit into our shared surroundings across an entire region.

Seeking harmony on a local level, the Salish and Kootenay tribes of the Flathead Nation in northwestern Montana recently decided to restore their forests nearly to pre-European conditions. That doesn't mean an end to logging on the 1.3-million-acre reservation, which stretches westward from the crest of the Mission Range. Historically, these reservation forests included a mixture of open, partially regrown, and ancient stands. Logging, together with prescribed fires, can be used to re-create that diversity. The difference is that the goal of the timber program is not to maximize revenue but to strengthen nature.

To complement a federal wilderness on the eastern slope of the Mission Range, the Flathead Nation established a 92,000-acre tribal wilderness on the western slope in 1982. During the late 1980s, they declared a wilderness buffer zone of 23,000 acres. The tribes also maintain a 59,000-acre primitive area and a 27,000-acre scenic river corridor. At the peak of the summer hiking and fishing season, they put 10,000 acres around McDonald Peak off-limits to avoid disturbing grizzlies that gather on the high talus slopes to lick up swarms of army cutworm moths and ladybird beetles, commonly called ladybugs. All of these measures also help protect west-slope cutthroat trout, which have become rare in the Rockies, and bull trout, listed in 1999 as a threatened species.

The wilderness and recreation specialist for tribal lands is Tom McDonald, a descendant of Salish, Nez Perce, and Chippewa-Cree people; French and Norwegian folk; and the Scottish immigrant Angus McDonald, for whom the mountain is named. "We have not set aside wilderness and primitive areas in the hope of luring tourists and making money," he says. "We still have strong religious beliefs about sharing and showing respect for everything." Everything includes mountains, streams, rocks, and winds as well as wildlife. All of them have histories kept alive in the stories of tribal elders, and all of them are imbued with a spirit.

I am beginning to understand the Native view: this is an animate landscape, a cultural landscape—anything but a collection of objects separate from and secondary to humankind. Brian Lipscomb, the tribal manager of wildlife, recreation, and conservation, tries to amplify for me: "When I pray over an animal, it is not like white people think. I am praying to the Creator—the same One you know—to allow that animal to help me in whatever way the Creator sees fit. Our culture is tied to animals and other natural resources. If we lose those resources, we don't have a tribe. The United States as a whole is starting to come to that realization, I think. When you take something, you must give something back."

THE SWAN VALLEY runs between the Mission and Swan Ranges, the western edge of the brawny Bob Marshall Wilderness complex. Though it is sparsely populated, homesites, other developments, and the Swan highway are compressed along its narrow bottomlands, forming a long barrier to animal movements—

an ecological fault line. If it becomes too hard to cross, the wildlife community of the Mission Range, which includes one to two dozen grizzlies, will be stranded. Recovery officials are concerned that, like so many other small subpopulations, these bears will disappear over time despite the best efforts of Flathead Nation managers. Relying heavily on computer-generated maps of key habitats and human influences, USFWS biologists have made a top priority of securing corridors across the Swan Valley through conservation easements and other agreements with private landholders—with some success.

"Lynx are long-distance dispersers as surely as grizzlies are," I hear from John Squires of the University of Montana, who works at the Rocky Mountain Research Station in Missoula. "Lynx readily move between the Swans and the center of the Bob Marshall Wilderness," Squires tells me. "In 1985, a female was documented traveling almost 200 miles from Montana to Radium Hot Springs in British Columbia."

Studies such as his, based in the Swan Valley, were few before 1998, when the lynx was proposed for listing as a threatened species. Information is only just starting to trickle in, but researchers have learned this much: The long-legged, tassel-eared cats with thick fur on the soles of wide feet for staying atop deep snow are very sparsely distributed. In the Rockies, they tend to be associated with mature, high-elevation forests of mixed conifers that offer snowshoe hares and red squirrels to dine on. Thirdly, as Squires informs me, "The lynx populations in the U.S. that are most persistent seem to be those with connections to Canada."

On a spring night, you can often hear the birds for which the Swan Valley is named migrating high overhead on their way to Canadian breeding grounds. Still more tundra swans, along with a few trumpeters, follow the Rocky Mountain Front, riding the winds that flow east off the divide. My wife, Karen, and I meet the flocks as they settle down to rest for a while on the waters of Freezout Lake Wildlife Management Area, maintained by the Montana Department of Fish, Wildlife and Parks on the edge of the plains. We estimate 10,000 swans and at least 300,000 snow geese beside them, all white as the heights of the Bob Marshall Wilderness in the background. Each morning and evening, while gusts burnish the waters and the swans tip bottom-up to graze aquatic plants, the snow geese arise with cries and clattering wings and then swirl down like a spring blizzard onto stubbled fields nearby, to feed on leftover barley and wheat.

Soon after the swans pass through in early April, mergansers arrive to claim territories on sections of mountain rivers where currents are swift but smooth. Where the water twists white, harlequin ducks take over, plunging through rapids to feed on insect larvae, bobbing their heads in ritual displays, pattering to chase off rivals, and frequently hopping out onto midstream rocks to preen.

Males, patterned red and slaty blue with black stripes and white dots, stand out like early tourists in Hawaiian shirts. But by June, the drakes have returned to the seacoast, while the hens remain, muted brown huddles of feathers on nests tucked along the riverbank. Newly arrived human visitors have no inkling of the extravagant show that so recently played to the melting mountainsides.

On a summer day in Glacier National Park, I watch a female harlequin lead her brood through a quiet, fir-shaded pool on the side of a creek. The last duckling in line strays, gets captured by the current, and is swept away, tumbling over partly submerged stones. An eddy spins the baby close enough to calmer shore waters for it to skitter out of trouble and return to its family by scrambling overland.

What doesn't kill you counts as a lesson. It is supposed to make you stronger. I try to take comfort in this thought later in the day while trying to negotiate passage up a layer of limestone that juts out over a thousand-foot drop. I would rather reach summits the easy way, but the topography of the Rockies doesn't always provide one. At the top, I plant my rear end on the Pacific slope and my daypack on the Atlantic side and give thanks for being alive in a world that includes a thick sandwich and cookies.

Compared to Y2Y's northern terrain, its southern approaches may seem a bit like Europe—largely reshaped by development, its wildlands reduced to fragments. Yet compared with most of the rest of the lower 48 states, the southern Y2Y terrain looks more like the Yukon. Wyoming, Idaho, and Montana together only hold around 2.2 million people, about as many as metropolitan Cleveland. Close to half the acreage of these mountain states is public domain. Owned equally by all U.S. citizens, it can be made to serve the nation in any way thought best. Will the section along the Rockies be valued chiefly as a source of raw materials for more crowded regions, or as a repository of wild places and lives? Or, following the Y2Y conservation vision, as a landscape in which carefully thought-out designs for stewardship assure a supply of both types of resources indefinitely? Between the power of computer chips, the human mind, and mother nature, all things seem possible. Especially from this vantage point.

Farther down the ridge, another climber is surveying the realm below. A master climber. I don't know why mountain goats stare from conspicuous high points for such long spells. Eagles are the only predators up here. They pose little threat to an adult. A goat searching for members of its band should be able to find them with a glance or two. Maybe mountain goats gaze out lingeringly from the crown of the continent for the same reason some people say whales leap and harlequin ducks repeatedly ride a set of rapids: because they can. Me, I'm looking north along the Divide at the peaks marching on into Canada. Because I can, I will follow and pay my respects. ◆

FOLLOWING PAGES:
MAMMOTH HOT SPRINGS
Geologic turbulence underlies the tranquil beauty of Yellowstone's Mammoth Hot Springs. Although park geysers and boiling pools claim worldwide fame, dramatic thermal features can be found scattered throughout the Rocky Mountains. No surprise, since they arise from the same stresses and strains deep within the Earth's crust that built the mountain ranges of the Y2Y region and continue to uplift them today.

ROARING MOUNTAIN

Window on our planet's internal workings, Yellowstone's Roaring Mountain bellows steam from myriad fumaroles and fissures, continually reworking the landscape. Offering bare ground and forage all through winter's coldest months, such thermal areas aid the survival of animal populations on the high and snowy Yellowstone Plateau.

GRAND PRISMATIC SPRING AND OBSIDIAN CREEK

In Yellowstone, mineral deposits encrusting fallen twigs texture Obsidian Creek (right), while the living colors of Grand Prismatic Spring (left) result largely from microbes that flourish in boiling, sulfurous pools. These miniscule organisms may be the most valuable wildlife that Yellowstone protects. One heat-tolerant bacterium discovered in the park has greatly improved genetic engineering techniques; others can help clean up toxic wastes. Still others offer a potential glimpse of the conditions under which life arose on Earth.

FOLLOWING PAGES:
SHOSHONE N.F.

Protective bulwark for a precious commodity, a mother grizzly like this seldom reproduces before the age of five or six and generally gives birth only every second or third year.

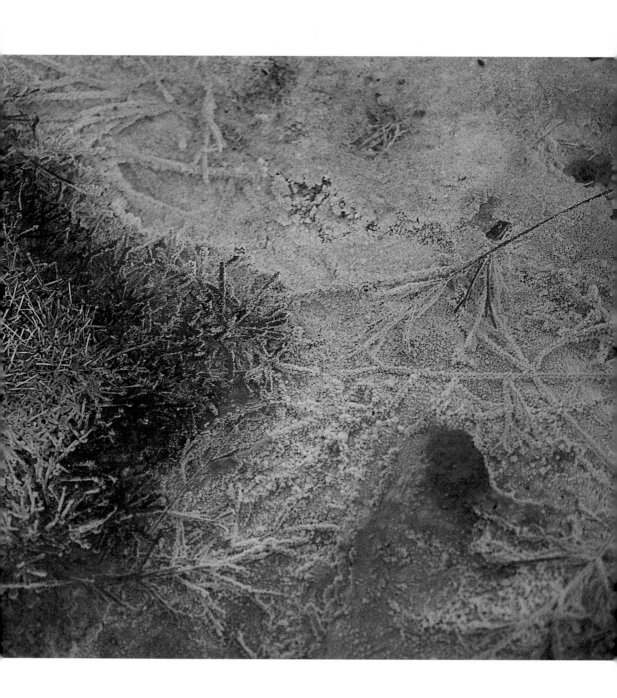

GREATER YELLOW-STONE ECOSYSTEM
Hunters like these young red foxes tussling beside their den can affect populations of birds, rodents, and other prey species. Similarly, the browsing preferences of moose (opposite) can impact the proportions of meadow, brush, and forest habitats.

FOLLOWING PAGES:
LAMAR VALLEY
Bovine with breakneck speed, a one-ton bison can reach 35 miles per hour. Yellowstone holds the only continuously surviving herds in the U.S. A slightly larger, woolier race known as wood bison survived in Canada and has been reintroduced to Y2Y.

GRAND TETON N.P.
Wyoming's granitic
Teton Range includes
12,605-foot Mount
Moran and 11 others
above 12,000 feet.
Reflecting this area's
huge snowfalls and
often sudden
snowmelts, Pilgrim
Creek swells to flood
stage (opposite). Thanks
to the strong work ethic
of beavers, however,
ponds and streams
across the Rockies hold
more water for more of
the year than would be
possible without these
rodents' dams. The
marshy margins of such
wetlands support nesting
waterfowl and also
nurture willow, dogwood
brush, and other essen-
tial moose chow.

ST. MARY LAKE, GLACIER N.P.

Daylight born just moments earlier strikes stone layers more than a billion years old in Montana's Glacier National Park. Uplifted from the floor of Precambrian oceans to heights now nearly two miles above sea level, the limestone and argillite rock strata on display here contain stromatolites—mats of fossilized algae and bacteria that represent some of the first organic structures on Earth. To witness mountain goats and bighorn sheep walking across them is to celebrate the enduring power and inventive-ness of life.

LOGAN PASS

Temporarily parked on the Continental Divide, a mountain goat shedding its winter coat joins human visitors in Glacier National Park's Logan Pass lot. Attracted to natural sources of mineral salts during late spring and summer, the wild mountaineers apparently find a tasty alternative in leaking engine coolants and transmission fluids.

PREVIOUS PAGES:
GLACIER N.P.

Not far from Logan Pass, the meltwaters of McDonald Creek flow by some of the nation's easternmost groves of western red cedar and western hemlock.

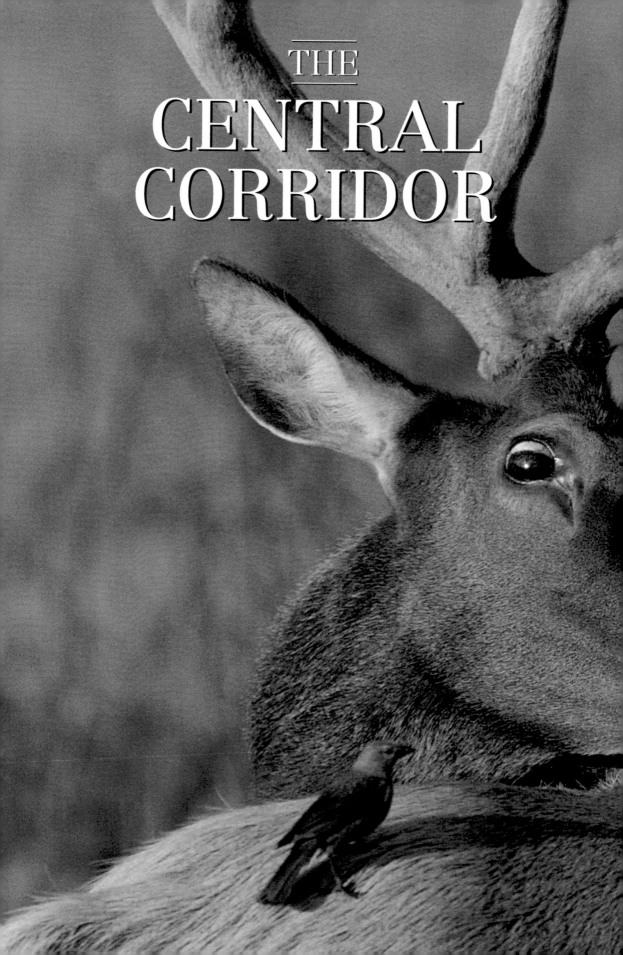

THE
CENTRAL
CORRIDOR

BANFF NATIONAL PARK ◆ KOOTENAY
NATIONAL PARK ◆ YOHO NATIONAL PARK
◆ MOUNT REVELSTOKE NATIONAL PARK
◆ GLACIER NATIONAL PARK ◆ PURCELL
WILDERNESS CONSERVANCY ◆ GOAT RANGE
PROVINCIAL PARK ◆ MOUNT ASSINIBOINE
PROVINCIAL PARK ◆ JASPER NATIONAL PARK
◆ WILLIAM A. SWITZER PROVINCIAL PARK
◆ WILLMORE WILDERNESS PROVINCIAL PARK
◆ MOUNT ROBSON PROVINCIAL PARK
◆ KAKWA PROVINCIAL PARK

**BOW VALLEY,
BANFF N.P.**

"Need help with that?"
a brown-headed
cowbird seems to say
from its front-row
perch atop a grooming
elk. Before Europeans
introduced cattle, such
avian companions
would have been more
aptly described as
buffalobirds. They often
feed around ungulates'
feet, catching insects
stirred up from the
ground. By hitching
rides on furry backs,
they find extra food in
the form of ticks and
other parasites, aiding
the big animals' efforts
to keep their coats
in good shape.

THREE WEEKS AGO, in late February, I went with Rick Yates to survey lynx tracks in Glacier National Park, Montana, where he works as a biologist. Not far past a set of otter prints, I noticed something buried in the snow under my cross-country skis. It was the top of one of the telephone booths that summer tourists in T-shirts use to describe flower-filled meadows to the folks back home. Behind me, Yates schussed off the roof of the shuttered campground store, whose eaves formed a continuous slope with the snowpack on the lee side.

The core of the Rockies looks like this—a deep and drifted, crystalline white—far longer than it looks like anything else. But just as it begins to seem that warmth and color and fragrance have abandoned this part of the world for good, there will come some faint rumor of spring that suddenly fills you with reawakening memories and longings to the point of bursting, as though you were carrying around a secret too great to bear.

One week ago, Yates and I met again at the snowy edge of Lake McDonald, on the west side of Glacier. The sky was a broth of clouds sliding in from the distant coast. We couldn't tell whether they would bring more snow or start pouring rain, winter's rule was softening so fast. The cedar-hemlock forest gave forth sounds like someone whistling over the mouth of a jug—the unmistakable song of the varied thrush, the mountain forest counterpart of the thrush better known as the robin. Along the ice-trellised upper cliffs of Mount Brown passed the silhouettes of eagles. Goldens, Yates said, judging by the slight V of the six-and-a-half-foot wingspans; bald eagles hold theirs more level. They were sailing north along the Lewis Range, whose crest is the Continental Divide.

Yates explained that the big birds were making use of orographic lift, meaning the air flow that piles up against steep topography, just as surf does along a shore. More golden eagles hurtled out of cloud bellies, followed the same ridgeline, and then, one by one, tacked across the McDonald Valley to continue north up the Livingston Range. By early afternoon, we were counting a dozen an hour.

Today, March 20th, I am 80 miles north of Glacier in Alberta's Kananaskis Valley, east of the great divide and south of Banff National Park. The way the morning sunlight is banging off mountain ranges to both sides, this will soon be a solar oven set on high country spring. If there were a phone booth in the meadow before me, I might strip to my T-shirt and call someone about the butterfly I just saw.

"The first of the year," exclaims Peter Sherrington, a geologist and paleontologist who lives near Calgary and has arrived well before sunrise. "Not a mourning cloak…ah, an anglewing. Lovely." Not that he isn't keeping track of fliers at loftier altitudes. From this spot, he has tallied 250 golden eagles in a single hour and 849 in one day. It was another March 20th, in 1992, when Sherrington came here on a regular bird count for the Alberta Natural Heritage Program and first noticed all the eagles going by. Since then, he and volunteers keeping vigil for months on end have recorded as many as 6,000 eagles each spring and again each fall. With luck, today will bring them sighting number 50,000.

To find soaring eagles in the Y2Y region has always been easy. To recognize them as part of one of North America's grandest migrations was a lot harder, because this migration is spread out over time, and takes place largely at or above summit level, where eagles become specks in an awfully big sky. Or, as Sherrington puts it, "where ornithology meets particle physics." Aiming his telescope over Mount Lorette, he identifies a bird three miles distant and two miles up as an immature golden by the white streaks under its wings. "Easterners," he says, "have no idea how far you can see in this dry mountain air."

Golden eagles winter in high deserts and plains to either side of the Rockies, living off jackrabbits and black-tailed prairie dogs. As days lengthen, the raptors journey north, their flight paths braiding between the Continental Divide and parallel ranges. Breeding pairs begin to migrate as early as February; younger birds follow, with non-breeders still coming through in May. Sherrington figures that roughly 10,000 eagles make the trip, peeling off to set up territories from northern British Columbia through Alaska and possibly on into Siberia. Come autumn, they return with fledglings they have reared among cliff walls on the likes of marmot and ground squirrel cutlets, mountain sheep carrion, and weak or stillborn caribou calves.

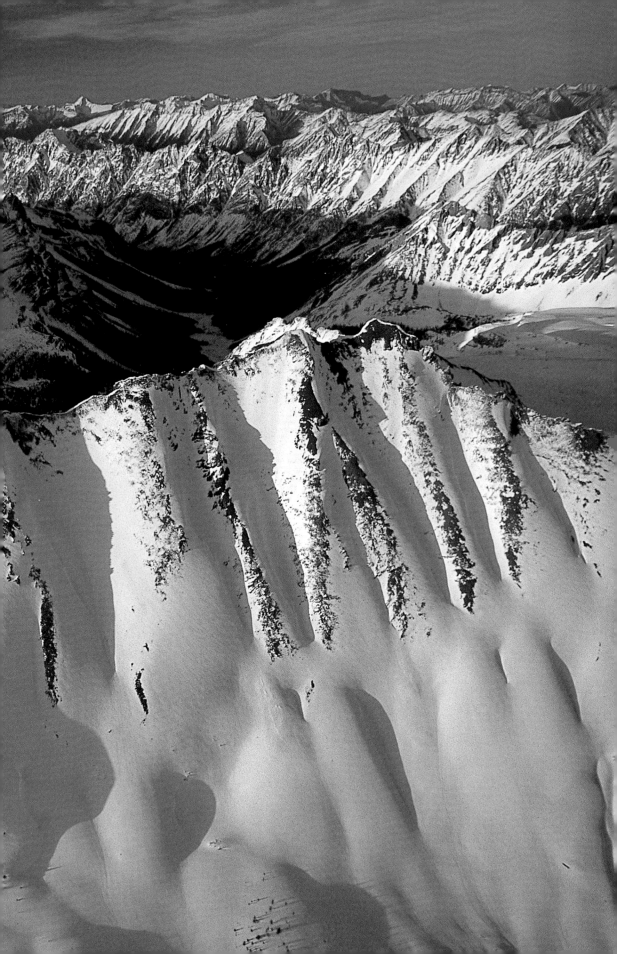

Eagles don't really fly on these journeys; that is, I have scarcely
seen one flap its wings today, and our count just shot past 350 birds.
They truly ride the winds. If air currents fade, they will settle onto
summits and ridgelines, just as they do each night, waiting to step
off into the next morning's sky. Right now, most are crossing the
Kananaskis Valley from the Fisher Range, moving northwest to
circle in the warmed air rising off sunstruck Mount Lorette.

"They have caught a nice little thermal pipe," Sherrington com-
ments. "I count five, six…no, nine birds in that boil." The total
reaches 25, which he pronounces "a splendid kettle of eagles." And
they keep ascending, spiraling up and up until they completely
disappear in the heavens. Where, you might say, ornithology meets
theology. But the eagles are just gaining altitude for the next stage, a
long glide across the Bow Valley.

Carved by past glaciers and overhung by modern ones, the
U-shaped valley enclosing the Bow River runs from Bow Lake, near
the divide, down the east side of Banff National Park and out onto
the Alberta prairie. Its easy contours provide passage both for the
Canadian Pacific Railway's main line and for the nation's main east-
west auto route, the Trans-Canada Highway. Motorists intent on just
getting from, say, Saskatoon to Vancouver abruptly find themselves
inside a national park surrounded by the most awesome assemblage
of peaks they may ever have seen in their lives. And the wildlife!
Coyotes and black bears dash across the roadway. Elk mothers with
calves stroll by shoppers in the Banff townsite while the bulls spar
from lawn to parking lot, clashing antler racks. No wonder the
animals are thriving, tourists think; just look at the country they live
in, tucked safely away in the care of park wardens.

Yet if I were a wild critter, Banff is not necessarily where I would
want to be right now. Out in Kananaskis, closer to the plains, elk are
grazing green shoots on bare ground; in Banff they are breaking
through soft snow up to their chests. Close to 97 percent of Banff
consists of subalpine and alpine habitats—colossal rock strata, ice,
and snow-smothered mountainsides. While mountain goats and
sheep can contend with long winters by keeping to south-facing
slopes and windblown knolls, most other animals seek the forested
valleys and floodplains that make up the park's remaining 3 percent.

Lowlands are scarce in the Rockies, and all the more precious.
Besides providing crucial winter range, they supply animals with natural thoroughfares. Conserving such wildlife corridors may be the
most important step toward maintaining the vitality of Y2Y ecosystems. And perhaps the most challenging one, since we humans tend
to claim bottomlands for ourselves—even within national parks.

In Banff, nine of every ten acres below the subalpine zone lie in
the Bow Valley. Traffic on the Trans-Canada Highway was killing so

many park animals—notably 1,600 elk since 1981—that stout game fences were finally built on either side of the asphalt. The barriers helped reduce roadkills but cost moose, elk, and deer their freedom to cross the valley. Elk moved lengthwise along the Bow instead, funneling toward the Banff townsite where the valley narrows. Since most wolves and other big carnivores avoid high levels of human activity, more and more elk have ended up lingering by this busy hub or between it and the town of Canmore, just beyond the park entrance.

The first two cougars I see at Banff are victims of high-speed collisions, stored in the freezer at the biology field office. There is a wolf, too, one of four recently killed by cars or trains in Yoho National Park, which adjoins Banff and, like it, is bisected by the Trans-Canada Highway and the Canadian Pacific Railway. Banff's new game-proof fencing edges the highway only where it has been enlarged to four lanes. Even there, it is not proof against beasts agile enough to climb over it or squirm through undercuts and tears, as the squashed coyote I pass must have done. The railroad line remains exposed, attracting hooved animals because the plowed tracks make for easier winter travel, while grain spilled from boxcars is an extra lure. And when carnivores come in to scavenge the carcasses of smashed ungulates, they get whacked in turn.

For the past several years, graduate student Carolyn Callaghan and her associates have followed the wolf population in and around Banff. Looking across the Bow Valley from a hilltop to the south, she tells me, "The park brochure says there are 75 wolves in Banff. We have less than half that many right now. In the last 15 years or so, 27 percent of the known wolf deaths have been from the railway, and 60 percent were on the highway. Just 5 percent were natural."

Her advisor, ecologist Paul Paquet, began monitoring predators here during the 1980s. He predicted that unless something was done about the compression of people, cars, trains, and wildlife, the number of wolves left in the Bow Valley by the year 2000 would be zero. He was discouragingly close to being right. "The Bow Valley used to have three packs," Callaghan says. "Now it has one. In 1996, three of the four pups born to this pack were lost to the highway. The next year, none of the five pups born survived, and we know at least one was hit on the railway. During 1998, the pack had no pups and was down to three members."

The highway also accounts for 35 percent of all coyote deaths in the Bow Valley. In 1998 alone, trains and automobiles killed 15 black bears here out of a population of a few dozen. The entire province of Alberta, which held 6,000 grizzlies earlier in the 20th century, now has around 750. More than one Canadian biologist tells me, "You Americans shouldn't count on us to resupply you with animals if you run out. We may have to come borrow some from you before long."

Banff has only 60 to 80 grizzlies, though it roughly matches Yellowstone in size. Grizz are much warier than black bears—so much so that the road here becomes a barrier to the north-south continuity of their population. No one has yet recorded an adult grizzly moving from one side of the Trans-Canada to the other.

"We can't even get an adult to live in the valley, much less cross it," says Mike Gibeau of the University of Calgary, who has helped lead the interagency East Slope Grizzly Bear Project for years. "The average female in the park is very small: 200 to 250 pounds. This is just generally poor habitat for grizzlies, and they are completely alienated from the best areas—the lower valleys."

Disturbances around all the picnic sites, campgrounds, villages, golf courses, resorts, and ski complexes crammed into the Bow Valley simply add up to more than many grizz can handle. Others tolerate the hubbub, yet if they are lured by garbage or groceries, or just hang around too close, they face capture and relocation—or execution. They also may amble downstream and wind up in trouble amid the subdivisions sprawling from Canmore. Development there is so close to choking off the natural routes for wildlife through the Bow Valley that some of the newer golf course fairways have been designated to double as travel corridors. There are even guidelines for how soon after, say, a cougar takes down a deer on the 10th green, parties can once again play through. Meanwhile, many residents of the Banff townsite feel overrun by elk and want them moved out.

In short, the tourist view of this park as a vast and undisturbed animal paradise is an illusion. Like so many Rocky Mountain reserves, Banff is as rugged as topography gets—and as biologically marginal as it is stupendous to behold. In the best living spaces Banff does offer, the same transportation corridor that pumps in human visitors also drains the vitality of the natural community by undermining the valley's function as a wildlife corridor. The conflict is proving especially harmful to big predators in one of the few parts of Canada where they are supposed to enjoy full protection. Rather than serving as a refuge whose surplus could resupply nearby range, the park has become a population sink.

The implications reach beyond the 49th parallel. Banff probably supplied the wolves that naturally recolonized the American West during the late 1970s. The packs of northern Montana, particularly the Glacier National Park ecosystem, and those from the southern portions of Alberta and British Columbia continue to form a metapopulation, exchanging members. A wolf seen in Montana's North Fork of the Flathead one month might be in the Bow Valley the next—and wind up as roadkill. Many of the region's grizzlies, other carnivores, and hooved wildlife have what amounts to dual citizenship as well. What helps or hinders their survival in one locale can influence every corner of the countryside sooner or later.

The proliferation of roads and high-speed traffic is one of the most serious problems facing wildlife anywhere—and one of the most widely ignored. Within Y2Y, 64 major roadways exist between west-central Wyoming and the middle of B.C. and Alberta, and the number of automobiles doubles every couple of decades. Wildlife managers worry that 2,000 to 3,000 vehicles per day on a road are enough to fragment animal populations and lead to declines. Banff's highway averages 14,000. In summer, the figure exceeds 20,000. Since wildlife needs its highways as surely as we need ours, one potential solution is to find better, safer ways for the two to intersect.

TONY CLEVENGER, an American scientist contracted by Banff Park, takes me along on his regular check of 24 possible passageways for large animals beneath the road. Most are where bridges span river channels. At each tunnel, he and several co-workers search for wildlife sign and carefully rake sections of dirt smooth so they can more easily pick out future tracks. Coyote pawprints are fairly common. Elk and deer hoofs mark some of the wider, more open routes. Among grizzlies and wolves, a few males go through now and again, but the females refuse. Under one bridge, we find fresh droppings. They are from *Homo sapiens.* Next to them is a message scrawled in the raked soil: TOO MUCH STUDY / NOT ENOUGH PROTECTION. When it comes to some mammal species, you can almost count on every individual approaching things a little differently.

Clevenger goes on to show me some of the 25 smaller passageways his team monitors—mainly drainage culverts. Not surprisingly, burrowing animals such as mice and weasels take to them fairly readily. The reactions of mid-size creatures are less predictable. We can see prints in the snow where a wolverine looked over an entryway and then shied back into the lodgepole pine woods.

I am eager to check out two additional crossings, which go not under but over the highway and represent something new in North America's annals of engineering. They are massive concrete bridges that are off-limits to people, built exclusively for four-legged traffic. Each is 160 feet wide, several hundred feet long, covered with rock and dirt, and planted with native trees and shrubs—an arch of habitat high above the asphalt. The twin causeways were completed in November of 1997. Poking at an old hoofprint, Clevenger says that dozens of deer and elk have ventured across since then. So have several cougars and black bears. No grizz or wolves as of March 1999, but the animals may need more time to adjust.

"I went to Greece last fall to see a new highway that bisects a remnant brown bear population near the border with Albania," Clevenger tells me. "They were building five miles of tunnels to bury the road and nine miles of viaducts as high as 80 feet off the ground. In all, they altered 40 percent of the length of the new highway, and this was for a group of maybe 25 bears."

In Canada, objections to the $3.3 million (U.S.) cost of the twin wildlife bridges nearly scuttled the project before it ever got underway. Premature and excessive, critics charged, adding that local animal populations were large enough to take care of themselves. It seems that wild creatures—and wild places—have to be on the verge of disappearing altogether before they are valued as priceless.

But not always. On the edge of Montana's Glacier National Park, mountain goats once had to cross U.S. Highway 2 to reach a riverside salt lick. Widening the road during the 1980s could have resulted in more goats being butted to death by cars, not to mention serious injury to drivers. Instead, planners called for an elevated road that left the salt-seekers plenty of room to clamber underneath, guided there by roadside fencing. A large parking space with a boardwalk was added so that motorists could watch the white mountaineers.

This happens to be one of the only known sites where goats from Glacier mingle with more southerly bands, which swim the Middle Fork of the Flathead River to reach the same lick. Now and then a goat may switch allegiance and follow a different group to new range. Thus, from human safety and enjoyment to goat gene flow, the highway re-design seems to be functioning splendidly.

Weeks after my visit to Banff, a wolf finally crosses one of the special wildlife bridges. Then, in the summer of 1999, an adult grizzly crosses an overpass. The next report I hear concerns the alpha female of the Bow Valley wolf pack: She has died in a collision with a train, as have some of her pups. In June, the alpha male of the first wolves to den in Grand Teton National Park in 50 years is killed on the highway near Moran Junction, Wyoming.

IT WILL TAKE TIME to measure the effectiveness of Banff's overpasses. But like the goat underpass in Glacier, they are already valuable as symbols. We certainly have the know-how to make highways permeable to wildlife. Those graceful green arches that now greet motorists on the Trans-Canada say that we are also finding the will.

"We need to get serious about more wildlife crossings," agrees Carmen Purdy, who represents a sportsmen's group in the East Kootenay region of southeastern B.C. "But we don't need to lock up any more huge areas for protection." A lifelong timberman, Purdy, like others in resource industries such as mining and ranching, is deeply suspicious of the Y2Y Conservation Initiative. "I think the thing is another land grab by preservationists," he declares. "They always say this is for our grandchildren. I say, Why? So they can't use the place either? You have to take people's livelihoods into consideration. All this push to turn the whole province into a closed area where you can skip along hillsides picking daisies and singing zip-a-dee-doo-dah is starting to piss people off."

Bill Bennett, a lawyer, former owner of a hunting guide business, and aspiring politician, adds, "When mills start closing and mines start cutting back, people get scared. Some say let's diversify the economy. Okay, but the easiest thing to do is to sell off our scenery, turn our open space into view lots, and there goes your wildlife habitat. Businessmen from Calgary and Vancouver are buying up all the Kootenay bottomlands they can."

A recreational honky-tonk is how Purdy describes the resorts and vacation homes beginning to line the Rocky Mountain Trench toward Radium Hot Springs, at the western entrance to Kootenay National Park. "It isn't loggers and miners that ruin the countryside," he says. "It's the dammers and ditchers and real estate developers."

Purdy and Bennett contend that going after timber and minerals actually improves habitat by opening up forests, while parks support relatively poor wildlife numbers. They have a point, in that reserves like Banff contain more high panoramas than crucial cold-weather range. Moreover, most parks have traditionally suppressed wildfire, a major source of food renewal for species that rely on grasses and shrubs. Although the road networks that come with logging and mining often leave animals more vulnerable to shooting, trapping, and general disturbance, this can—in principle—be handled by gates, tighter regulations, and stricter enforcement. There remain two issues. First, a lot of people treasure pristine backcountry, especially old, intact forests. Secondly, an array of species, from mushrooms and beetles to northern goshawks and mountain caribou call those deep woodland habitats home for at least part of the year and simply cannot thrive without them.

Driving west on the Trans-Canada from the Banff/Yoho/Kootenay complex for a couple of hours takes you through heavily logged timberlands to the Columbia Mountains of B.C. and two other national parks: Mount Revelstoke and Glacier. (This Glacier lies more than 200 miles from Montana's similarly named park, but is linked by remaining stretches of wildland.) The slopes of these parks wring so much precipitation from eastward-flowing air masses that their valley bottoms grow true rain forests. With western red cedar and western hemlock rising from a shadowy floor of mosses, ferns, and mold-softened windfalls, these woods seem magically transported from Vancouver Island. Farther uphill, however, *Continued on page 106*

Continued on page 106

THE CENTRAL CORRIDOR
MAJOR ISSUES

A wild heart with arterial problems, Alberta's Bow River Valley harbors tons of traffic both wild and human. It contains more than 90 percent of the bottomlands used by Banff's wintering animals, and serves as a primary wildlife corridor for migration and movement through extremely rugged terrain. At the same time, however, the Trans-Canada Highway brings an average of 14,000 vehicles a day speeding through this floodplain, while trains on the Canadian Pacific Railway main line rumble along a parallel route. A trip across the valley thus becomes a potentially lethal challenge for even the fleetest of beasts.

THE CENTRAL CORRIDOR

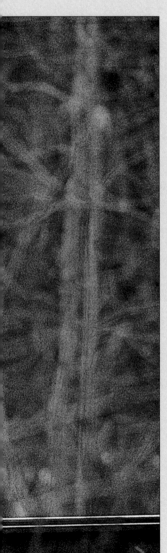

On the wrong track: Elk such as this "spike bull," or yearling male (far left), commonly follow the path of the Canadian Pacific Railway. Plows keep the main line nearly snow free in winter, while grain shaken loose from hurtling boxcars provides another attraction. So many hooved travelers are struck by trains that predators and scavengers regularly prowl the tracks—and become casualties in turn. Where the line runs through Banff and adjoining Yoho National Parks, losses of wolves and bears have been sufficiently high to jeopardize populations within the very lands intended to safeguard them. Why creatures with such superb reflexes are so vulnerable is unclear; even keen-eyed ravens, among the wariest of opportunists, get whacked by trains.

THE CENTRAL CORRIDOR

Building bridges to the future: The roads of Y2Y turn not only common forest species like deer, but also higher altitude creatures such as mountain caribou and bighorn sheep (right) into highway paté. Local carnivores feel the automobile's impact as well—literally. Late in 1997, Banff unveiled a fresh alternative: broad overpasses across the Trans-Canada Highway, designed for four-footed traffic. Built of concrete, covered with dirt and rocks and natural vegetation, these arches of habitat are off-limits to humans—except researchers, who regularly survey them for animal tracks (far right). At a cost of $1.65 million each, they tell of a society willing to invest seriously in long-term coexistence with its wildlife.

For sale: Grt 6BR, 4$\frac{1}{2}$ BA w/ mtn vu. Just east of Banff, the rapid spread of the town of Canmore (left) is beginning to plug off key wildlife migration routes in the scenic Bow Valley. As a compromise to shutting down development, planners suggest that new golf courses (above) serve as substitute corridors—with fences to keep wildlife off the greens. From Yellowstone to the Yukon, residents increasingly ponder how to enjoy the flow of wildness that makes their home special—without interrupting it.

Even in twilight, it's not hard to see why folks want to live in Banff—or why

animals that rely on valley lowlands for habitat and corridors are becoming less free.

the Ice Age still appears to rule. Around 400 glaciers grind and ooze through the 540 square miles of B.C.'s Glacier National Park, established in 1886. Even in mid-June, avalanches remain a danger, and I can scarcely find a trail that has melted out from under the deep snowpack despite afternoon temperatures rising into the 80s. So I stop at Canyon Hot Springs, yet another Y2Y example of water superheated by the deep forces associated with mountain building, and sign up to travel the very lowest terrain possible. That would be the Illecillewaet River, via rubber raft. Alongside tourists from England and Germany, I paddle hard through churning chutes, then relax where the water does and let the boat spin in the current while blue sky spiked with white mountains revolves overhead.

Mount Revelstoke National Park, set aside in 1914 about 15 miles west of Glacier, is almost as snowbound. Its 104 square miles would scarcely be enough to hold any wide-ranging mammal year-round, even if the place were ice free. Until recently, a lot of bears spent more time in and around the nearby logging community of Revelstoke, attracted by the local dump and other garbage sources. Between 1986 and 1996, when this food supply was finally cleaned up, at least 311 black bears and 120 grizzlies were captured and either relocated or killed. In other words, any benefit the animals gained from having parklands to roam was more than counteracted by the fact that the parks are ecologically incomplete and their human neighbors were operating by a whole different set of rules.

Bruce McLellan, habitat research biologist for the B.C. Ministry of Forests, works out of Revelstoke. A leading authority on grizzlies, he fears more for the future of mountain caribou, the unique race of woodland caribou endemic to these wet ranges west of the Continental Divide. Their lives depend upon old-growth forests, specifically upon the lichens that drape tree branches in cool, moist, undisturbed groves. "Mountain caribou are our spotted owls," McLellan says as we travel the countryside. "Because they use the kind of forest that is most valuable commercially, their requirements are directly at odds with the annual timber harvests allowed."

North of the Trans-Canada Highway in the Glacier/Mount Revelstoke area, the mountain caribou population is more or less continuous. As you go south, you find 18 here, 25 there, a few more in the Purcell Wilderness Conservancy, a dozen others near Goat Range Provincial Park, and so on. Finally, the sole U.S. population, totaling about 30, hangs on in the Selkirk Mountains of northern Idaho, where roads and clearcuts surround the last ancient woodlands.

In McLellan's opinion, "It's a classic study in conservation biology, with a shrinking population becoming further and further fragmented into island populations that probably won't make it on their own. Both grizzlies and mountain caribou are in a pattern typical of the late stages of extinction toward the southern end of their range. But there are only 2,500 of these caribou left in the world."

All the more reason to find ways of linking these last islands together, I think, as I turn back toward the Continental Divide and Mount Assiniboine Provincial Park. From this former stronghold of the Stoney Indian tribe, I pass into neighboring Kootenay National Park, where Indians once gathered ochre for painting themselves and their tipis. The pigment still occurs in a series of mineral springs that emerge through volcanic-looking mounds of iron oxide and iron hydroxide. Called Paint Pots, these burbling pools are mountain cold. The Stoneys believed a big animal spirit—a thunder spirit—made its home here, and that when people came to the pools, they would sometimes hear the sound of a flute or war songs but could never see the source. Squatting down by the lip of one spring, I close my eyes and listen. I hear the drum of my own heart after an uphill walk, and the whistled chatter of ruby-crowned kinglets and mountain chickadees in the pines. The wind wheezes through the branches, and, after a while, I can make out the distinct voice of each rivulet running from the springs to the stream. Spirit enough, I think, before a falling pine cone breaks my reverie and I move on.

FROM KOOTENAY, my route leads back to Banff, then north into neighboring Jasper National Park via the Icefields Parkway. If there is a more scenic drive on a smooth road anywhere through the great mountain halls of the world, it must be a secret. Here you motor for hour upon high country hour among whole horizons of blue ice or layered stone or raw talus; you pass moraines at the feet of glaciers, titanic crags blocked from the sun by still higher massifs, mountain goats, elk, and bighorn sheep visiting mineral licks, lakes turquoise with rock flour freshly ground off the summits and cliffs. No four-wheel drive or hiking required. No previous experience necessary to take on a seemingly limitless procession of topography-in-the-making at the crown of the continent. All you need is a durable rump.

Lacking one, I get out after crossing the North Saskatchewan River at the start of its long voyage eastward, and stretch my lungs on the path up to Parker Ridge overlooking Saskatchewan Glacier. The trailside clusters of spire-shaped subalpine fir and spruce exude the bittersweet, resinous fragrance that, to me, promises fine rambling. For this is the scent of treeline. It wafts from the extra thick sap these survivors need to keep from freezing at their high outposts. Heavy wax on their needles serves the same purpose and counters drying from the mountain winds and high-altitude sun. On the firs, those needles stand upright like bristles on a hairbrush to catch and hold snow, adding another layer of insulation between living tissues and the extreme environment.

For all their adaptations, the trees quickly become smaller as I follow the path's switchbacks uphill. Soon, the only reminder of the forests that coat so much of this region are a few firs growing not so much upward as sideways, dwarfed and prostrated before the elements. Dwarf willow, mountain heather, yellow mountain heath, mountain avens, wooly everlasting, white globeflower; all have taken on a low profile to survive. Yet these ingredients of alpine tundra huddle together into an improbably luxuriant cushion that lets me take off my boots and continue barefoot toward the ridgeline.

Even the chipmunks here come in compact size. Known as least chipmunks, they are busy harvesting flower tops and probing after the insects burrowed into the thick cushion's stored warmth. Several white-tailed ptarmigan have the same idea. Having migrated from far to the south to nest above treeline, a pair of American pipits hunt among the sedge clumps by a meltwater pool, their movements habitually punctuated by wags of tailfeathers.

As I cross the ridgetop, my gaze lifts from the micro-worlds of tundra toward the Columbia Icefield, straddling the divide like a minor polar ice cap. This showpiece of Jasper Park spawns 34 glaciers and feeds rivers bound for three different oceans. The five-and-a-half miles of crevasse-riddled ice spilling like a slow-motion flood through the valley before me is Saskatchewan Glacier.

Not far beyond the rubble heaps of its terminal moraine, trees begin again, reclaiming a fan of talus between upper and lower cliff walls. Something unexpectedly bright shows among the dark foliage, and although it is miles away, I can tell that it is moving. I figure the object's light color plus the steep location add up to a mountain goat. Flopping down on a bed of heather belled with tiny, white flowers, I prop my telescope on my daypack and scan the far site. What emerges is not one animal but two, a mother grizzly and her cub, the sun glinting brightly off their silver-tipped fur. What they are doing or why they climbed such steep terrain are questions for which only they and these mountains have answers.

THE NEXT DAY I loop from Jasper to William A. Switzer Provincial Park and on to Alberta's immense Willmore Wilderness Provincial Park—more Y2Y heartland, continuing north where Jasper leaves off. A major entryway to Willmore is guarded by Hell's Gate, also known as Sulphur Gate, a cliff of stygian-looking volcanic rock where the glacial gray Smoky River meets the darker waters of the Sulphur River. While it all sounds a bit infernal, the reality is quite different. Geraniums and wild rose petals flourish in aspen glades on the hillsides, and horsemen are packing their mounts for a trip westward toward the divide through mountain scenery that seems like a preview of the Promised Land.

The next time I travel the Icefields Parkway I turn northwest, taking Highway 16 from the Jasper townsite. In this direction the park meets B.C.'s Mount Robson Provincial Park at Yellowhead Pass, named for the blond Iroquois fur trader who discovered this route around 1827. Mount Robson is the tallest peak in the Canadian Rockies, at 12,972 feet. Yet Robson Valley, which leads north between the Rockies and the Cariboo Mountains on the west, is low and broad, another segment of that great fault line running in tandem with the divide through much of Y2Y: the Rocky Mountain Trench.

About 25 percent of the Robson Valley, sometimes referred to as the Upper Fraser Valley, is cedar-hemlock woodland. Here, right next to the snowy crest of the continent, is the core of the largest interior temperate rain forest in the world. As if its green tangles do not already resemble a coastal setting closely enough, sea-grown salmon splash in its waters. Roughly 10 percent of the chinook in the Fraser River system, B.C.'s major drainage, spawn in the Robson Valley. By the time they near Mount Robson, they have swum 800 miles from the Pacific. As they lie dying in the shallows afterward, their bodies are snatched up in powerful jaws to become sinew and winter fat of Rocky Mountain grizzly, just as salmon in Idaho once used to be.

Mount Robson's cedar-hemlock stands are mainly old-growth. Most of the big trees have seen a few centuries come and go; some have stood watch for more than a thousand years. These magnificent geezers, gnarled, lightning-scarred, busted by winds, and partly hollowed by rot, are communities unto themselves, with black bears sleeping inside them and mosses, liverworts, ferns, huckleberry bushes, shrub maples, and even respectable-size spruce trees growing from their sides.

Rick and Julie Zammuto, whose home and garden near Crescent Spur are surrounded by these ancients, explain that certain cedar-hemlock stands have kept their basic structure far longer than usual, because they escaped burning and other natural events that would cause plant succession to start over. Suspended in a perpetual climax stage for much of the post-glacial era, these are beyond old-growth. The term for them, the Zammutos tell me, is antique forests.

Interior cedar-hemlock woodlands have the highest diversity of native trees in the province—a dozen kinds of conifer along with an assortment of deciduous species such as poplar and birch. This isn't very impressive compared to the spectrum of trees in tropical rain forests. Yet, surprisingly, the overall biological diversity of an old-growth temperate rain forest, including all its microscopic life-forms, may equal or exceed that of the tropics. More amazing, its total biomass—as high as 600 metric tons per acre—can be three to eight times greater than that of a tropical rain forest.

The difference is on and under the ground. Tropical rain forest soils are thin and leached of nutrients. Beneath an ancient cedar-hemlock stand, however, lies a deep, slowly decomposing layer of organic litter riddled with life-forms that range from beetles to worms. Now weave in among the fallen logs and humus an estimated 5,000 species of mycorrhizal fungi—the long, thin, microscopic threads that attach to root hairs and bring the host plant extra water and nutrients in return for a bit of carbohydrate. By contrast, a tropical rain forest might have no more than a dozen species of mycorrhizal fungi.

A different symbiotic relationship between fungi and another group of organisms—in this case, algae or cyanobacteria—produces lichens. They abound in interior old-growth forests, particularly the antique stands. "We've had specialists come to study them from as far as Europe," Rick Zammuto tells me. "They have recorded something like 60 lichen species so far, including ocean-edge kinds never before found inland. Other kinds had only been recorded in places like South America until people looked here."

The grizzly and black bears, salmon and bull trout, pileated and black-backed woodpeckers, northern goshawks, and barred owls moving through these forests also contribute to their diversity. So do woodland caribou, which come to the Robson Valley to calve. Like the mountain caribou race, woodland caribou in general have been declining in the Canadian Rockies as a result of forest fragmentation. Bull trout and salmon have also dwindled, as logging and roadbuilding have smothered their spawning beds with silt and caused the waters to warm to unhealthy levels.

Timbering has been the region's economic mainstay for years. A tremendous amount of clearcutting has already taken place along this portion of the Rocky Mountain Trench, and plans from the Ministry of Forests once called for continuing it until virtually all the cedar-hemlock stands in the Robson Valley were logged off.

While the grand, old geezers remained as silent as ever, Rick Zammuto got busy on their behalf. Hunched over a computer console in his remote cabin, he applied the principles of conservation biology to map areas that he felt should be spared in order to ensure connections of forest habitat up and down the valley and across from the Rockies to the Cariboos. He, Julie, and the Save-The-Cedar League they founded were roundly denounced by the logging lobby. But Rick seems to draw reserves of strength directly from the ancient woodlands. Nor is Julie, the daughter of "Wild Bill" Ezinicki, longtime holder of the record for the most fights in professional hockey, inclined to just sit back and take what comes.

The struggle came to a head as the B.C. Ministry of Environment policies were changing to emphasize protection of the province's rich biological diversity. In concert with local conservationists and national groups, the Zammutos helped spur the government to set aside a dozen key areas of forest on public lands as new provincial parks or additions to existing ones. At the same time, nearly half a million acres between Robson Valley and Willmore Wilderness became Kakwa Provincial Park, expanding the already impressive sequence of reserves along the Continental Divide. None too soon. To get to Kakwa, I drive close to fifty miles on a rough gravel road through logged areas, including one clear-cut that must be a dozen miles long.

Interestingly, the hosts at the central campground in the new park are Richard and Betty-Ann Penner, whose regular jobs depend upon timber. Betty-Ann works for the Ministry of Forests as a scaler, measuring and recording the loads brought in by trucks from cutting sites. Richard is a millwright at one of the three pulp mills in Prince George.

"There is no way the companies can make the kind of big profits they used to in the heyday of logging," Betty-Ann tells me. "We need to develop more secondary wood industries."

"The timber we used to throw away as waste during logging operations was just unbelievable," Richard admits. "But we've really improved over the last 30 years. The pulp mills and sawmills are leaner, trimmer, more efficient. But with the government setting lower quotas for harvest, Prince George had 18 percent unemployment last year. That's the thing that gets people nervous about Y2Y: you're talking about their incomes. We all can't live on tourism. Not up here; we're pretty isolated from the southern part of the province. Guys not only worry about their jobs but about their right to go hunting and fishing, four-wheel driving, snowmobiling, or doing whatever they want out in the woods on public land."

Yet here the Penners are, volunteering weeks of their time to help a newly formed park and key Y2Y addition. But then Kakwa, still in the process of preparing for visitors, is hardly the type of reserve from which local folks feel excluded. Snowmobiles are permitted, as is trapping. Hunting will be allowed on all but a third of the acreage. And the prime commercial timber is mostly outside its boundaries.

Meanwhile, Kakwa has every age of rock from Precambrian to Recent, in bands that dip and warp and bend again, sometimes projecting straight up, sometimes reflecting pink and orange light over avalanche slopes. There is as much fresh grizzly bear sign around as I have seen anywhere in the Rockies. Woodland caribou dot the open slopes below a snowfield. The name Kakwa comes from the Cree word for porcupine, and I see signs of their gnawing by the cook shack and on the outhouse door. Any of these animals might have picked gentler terrain in which to go about their lives but nowhere lovelier, and I know all of us gathered at the campground agree on that. ◆

FOLLOWING PAGES:
YOHO NATIONAL PARK
Measured against the immensities of sun, stone, and sky, a solitary human figure can seem a fleeting shadow. Peaks of the Canadian Rockies offer us much, from exercise to nature to immersion in pure beauty. Yet perhaps the most important thing we can take away is humility. For, to a mountain, all the nations of history with all their great clangor and monuments to themselves merely come and go like nature's seasons.

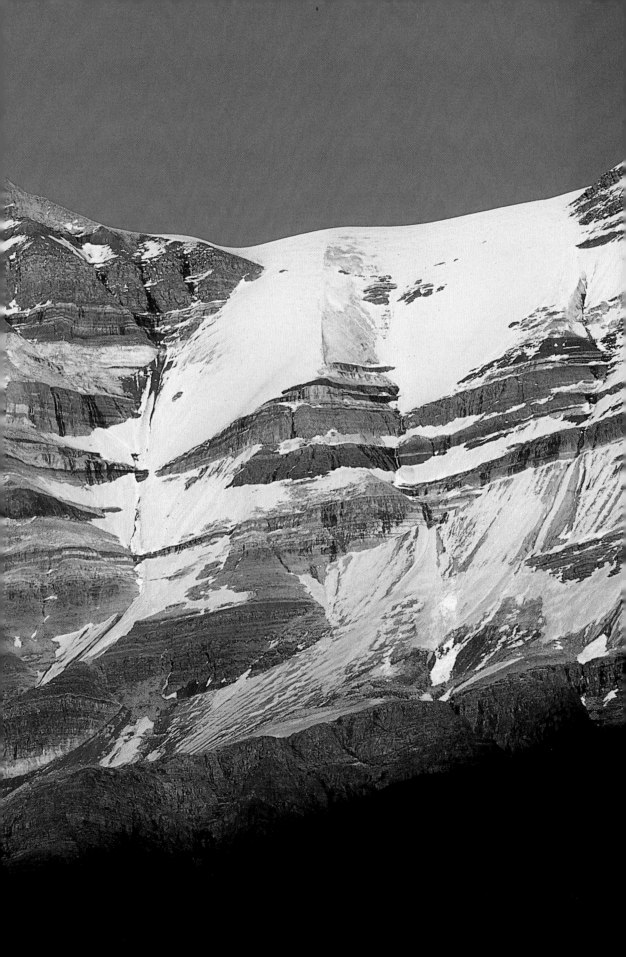

**GLACIER PEAK
RIDGE, YOHO N.P.,
AND MORAINE
LAKE, BANFF N.P.**
Opportunities for
reflection abound
near the crest of the
continent at places
like Lake O'Hara Lodge
in Yoho (opposite)
and Banff's Moraine
Lake (above). In
today's increasingly
crowded and fast-
paced world, Canada's
parklands of the
Continental Divide pre-
serve plenty of elbow
room and remind us
of the pleasures of
lingering. For a small
entry fee—a tiny
fraction of what
psychologists or
self-help courses will
set you back—they
can knit together
fractured thoughts
and suffuse a soul
with peace. Think
about it; places
such as these may
be North America's
best bargains.

VERMILION RANGE, BANFF N.P.
Winter's white tapestry shapes forests directly, by striping them with avalanche tracks, and indirectly, by favoring cold-tolerant tree species. Lasting half the year or more, winter is the longest season by far in Y2Y, most of which lies above 3,500 feet.

FOLLOWING PAGES:
BOW VALLEY, BANFF N.P.
Winter conditions also strongly mold the ecoregion's native animals, like this bull elk in Banff. Studies show that prolonged snow and cold have a greater influence on ungulate numbers than all predation combined. Male elk have poorer survival rates than females, in part because they enter the snow season with fat reserves newly drained by the demands of battle and courtship during the autumn rut.

KANANASKIS VALLEY

Conservationist Peter Sherrington (left, with tripod) swaps information with visitors to Alberta's Kananaskis Valley. In 1992 he discovered a spectacular eagle migration along the mountaintops. He and others have since counted close to 6,000 every spring and fall. Most are goldens, like this white-patched youngster (above).

FOLLOWING PAGES:
KOOTENAY N.P.

No beauty in the eye of an ecologist, the ox-eye daisy is a Eurasian invader that displaces native plants.

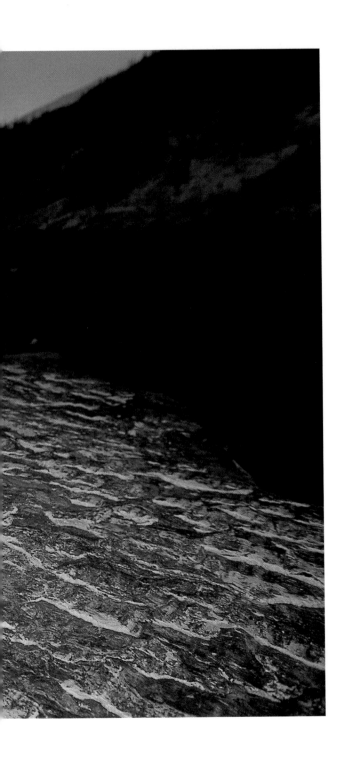

ATHABASCA GLACIER, JASPER N.P.

Casting only an illusion of warmth, the sun's last rays tint the textured surface of Jasper's Athabasca Glacier, one of 34 glaciers spawned by the Columbia Icefield. The Icefield straddles the divide like a minor polar ice cap and gives rise to rivers that ultimately find their way to the Pacific, Atlantic, and Arctic Oceans.

COLUMBIA ICEFIELD
Off into the wild,
blue, and chilly yonder,
climber Troy Kirwan
(opposite) negotiates
a crevasse in Banff's
portion of the Athabasca
Glacier. Over in Jasper,
a Japanese visitor
(above) inspects another
edge of the same ice
river. Hidden crevasses
have claimed the lives
of some unwary tourists,
but even the least
experienced can safely
explore the huge
Columbia Icefield in
specially equipped
park buses.

**THE RAMPARTS,
JASPER N.P.**

With one mountainous
ridge shadowing the
next, sky-high Y2Y runs
some 2,000 miles long
and up to 500 miles
wide. Formidable terrain
has long been the
Rockies' best defense
against extensive devel-
opment. But growing
pressures today demand
a comprehensive conser-
vation plan for this area.

SIRDAR MOUNTAIN, JASPER N.P.

As any eagle can show you, a six-foot wingspan makes travel a lot easier among the magnificently corrugated Rocky Mountains. Although cliff-nesting golden eagles are most common, bald eagles like the adult perched on this subalpine fir also occur, especially along the edges of rivers and lakes.

MIETTE RANGE, JASPER N.P.

Do you know where your children are? Mountain goat nannies always do. These two juveniles may be temporary playmates rather than siblings, for twins are rare among the Rockies' premier alpinists. The beginnings of winter coats are evident here, needed for the coming cold months when high country snows drift so deep that the 25- to 40-pound kids can no longer paw through them for forage and must feed instead in craters dug by their mothers. Severe winters can be particularly deadly, leaving no more than one or two youngsters out of every ten to greet the return of spring greenery.

THE
NORTHERN
REACH

NORTHERN ROCKY MOUNTAINS PROVINCIAL
PARK ◆ DENETIAH PROVINCIAL PARK
◆ MUNCHO LAKE PROVINCIAL PARK ◆ STONE
MOUNTAIN PROVINCIAL PARK ◆ WOKKPASH
RECREATION AREA ◆ MUSKWA-KECHIKA
WILDERNESS ◆ NISUTLIN RIVER DELTA N.W.A.
◆ NAHANNI NATIONAL PARK RESERVE
◆ TATLATUI PROVINCIAL PARK ◆ KWADACHA
WILDERNESS PROVINCIAL PARK
◆ TOMBSTONE RANGE TERRITORIAL PARK

PREVIOUS PAGES:
YUKON TERRITORY
Panting from summer's
relative heat, caribou
come well insulated
with a dense coat of
hollow hairs. On warm
days, herds of this
northernmost member
of the deer family
commonly lounge on
snowbanks, which also
help them avoid the
insect hordes that
inevitably bloom along
with the wildflowers.

IN THE LATE, amber light of evening in far northern British Columbia, Marcie Fofonoff sits on a gravel bar at the marshy edge of Denetiah Lake, balancing her dinner plate on her knees. "It's a good idea to add pepper or parsley flakes when you're cooking," she observes. Not for spice, but because the dark specks make it easier to ignore all the gnats and mosquitoes stuck in the food.

I lean back against a heap of gear and look past the cookfire at mirror images of peaks on the lake surface. Trout rise through them. These fish seem to be doing fine on insect fare. Lesser yellowlegs and other shorebirds probing the shallows for larvae also appear enthusiastic. Even the black and grizzly bears in the nearby forests may be licking up six-legged prey under rocks and logs. Figuring that I, too, am going to need all the energy I can gather, I fork in another mouthful of mixed protein and chew away.

Our camp—a couple of tarps strung over a cluster of sedge hummocks—lies deep in the backcountry among wave after wave of mountains. Though it is midsummer, the float plane that carried me here was dodging squalls of fresh snow among those peaks. For the next two weeks, photographer Ray Gehman and I, Marcie, her companion Wayne Sawchuk (a guide, trapper, and professional conservationist), and their longtime friend Reed Radley (a plant pathologist from Vancouver) will be leading a string of horses southeastward across high passes, swamps, canyons, and big rivers. When we reach our destination, another lake about 120 winding miles away, we still will be deep in backcountry among waves of mountains. You won't find much "front country" north of Prince George, B.C., apart from scattered outposts along the Hart and Alaska Highways. This is where the real bush begins.

From looking over maps of Y2Y's northern terrain, it's plain that exploring northern B.C. alone could take a couple of lifetimes. And more than three-quarters of the Yukon Territory is still essentially backcountry. Instead of dashing from place to place, I decided to choose just a few and immerse myself in them. For me, the unique rewards offered by the northern terrain have less to do with any particular spot than with greeting each new day amid horizons that as yet have no bounds.

Much of my current journey will be through the recently established Muskwa-Kechika wilderness, 11 million acres in size. Close to two-thirds of this reserve is set aside as special management areas in which any future development must be temporary and limited. The remaining third consists of fully protected zones. Some, such as Stone Mountain and Muncho Lake Provincial Parks and the adjoining Wokkpash Recreation Area, were established years ago next to the Alaska Highway. Others, including Northern Rockies and Denetiah Provincial Parks, are brand new and remote. We may be Denetiah's original tourists. For that matter, we will probably be the first non-hunting group to ever traverse the section of wildlands ahead.

What Ray and I are carrying out is a jaunt compared to the expedition that Marcie and Wayne have underway. They started from Dease Lake more than a hundred miles to the west a month ago and traversed the Stikine Ranges and then the Continental Divide in the Cassiar Mountains to reach Denetiah Lake. After our journey from the Cassiars across the Rocky Mountain Trench and through an outlying series of peaks to the Gataga River, they will forge on for another month and a hundred more miles over the Muskwa Ranges.

"How many places can you ride for three months without hitting a road?" Wayne asks as we hunker over coals in the twilight. He and Marcie have carried out other long journeys most years and cherish the sense of self-reliance and adventure that deepens each step of the way. "I guess the thing I like best in the world," Marcie says, "is riding down into a new valley with the wind in my face."

The next morning, we move out along the lakeshore: Four men and a woman; five riding horses and six pack horses; two saddleless, adolescent horses tagging along to learn the trade; two chest-high foals here to nurse, sprawl, and poke their noses into everything at camp; Trash, the dog rescued from a garbage bag as a baby; and of course our loyal retinue of biting bugs. By the following day, a steady rain settles in, and the route narrows to where we are either coaxing horses over fallen boulders or criss-crossing the stream that cut these steep canyonsides. The current is swift and deep in places. Holding my feet up free of the stirrups in case I have to leap clear, I watch Trash, pawing frantically for shore as he floats down and under my mount's belly.

Moose, wolf, and grizzly tracks incise the sandbars and mud. The deep woods shade a feathery carpet of horsetail rushes, which the bears

often graze. I hear a commotion up ahead where Wayne and Reed have been axing apart fallen trees to open a path. From the shouts I can make out, they have run into a grizz. I can't tell how the meeting is going. At the middle of the pack string, boxed in by spruce and birch, I have no idea where the bruin is. All I can do is hold tightly to my own horse's reins and try to keep the animals behind in order.

Peace returns as the bear vanishes into the alder brush. Farther along, the horses come upon bear droppings so full of orange-red buffaloberries that we call the mess pie filling. They merely sniff and move steadily on, and my trust in the bush-savvy of this four-legged crew rises another notch. At dusk, puzzled that I cannot recognize one of our mounts turned out to graze by a shallow lake, I discover that I am looking at a cow moose that has temporarily joined the horses, no more concerned about them than they are about it.

The Frog River runs deep and fast and is beginning to clear with the spring melt. Though close to swimming, our older horses make the far shore; the little ones get carried off into a tangle of submerged snags. A kind of aquatic rodeo featuring Wayne and his horse ensues, to free the foals and escort them to their whinnying mothers. Regrouped, we follow moose trails, mostly on foot, through a latticework of bleached and blown-down trees. The aftermath of a forest fire, it tells a tale not of devastation but of renewal. So many saplings have sprouted from the burn that I look up and find Wayne standing on his horse's rump like a circus rider, trying to see over the leaves and pick out a route.

More miles of blowdown and a few bogs later, we struggle across another serious river, the Kechika, and are soon rewarded with the first trail on which we can finally ride more than walk. Running north-south along a section of the Rocky Mountain Trench, this is what Native Americans call Atse Dene Tunna, or Trail of the Ancient Ones, used for thousands of years before whites renamed it the Davie Trail.

They were prospectors, mainly, headed by horseback, hobnailed boot, snowshoe, and dogsled for the Klondike gold fields of the western Yukon Territory. In their rush, they left little trace. Patrols of Royal Canadian Mounted Police kept the way open for some time afterward. In modern times, the Davie Trail has been traveled infrequently, mainly by hunting parties and Kaska Indian trappers. Yet it remains clear for miles at a stretch, meandering through dry forest along the edge of a benchland. I can't think of a finer place to loaf in a saddle and watch the countryside rock by, the Cassiars high and thick in the west while the formidable escarpments of the Muskwa Ranges tower all along the eastern skyline. But taking in alpine vistas is not the most memorable part; being in the heart of an equally grand and wild valley is.

Lowlands this wide and accommodating are generally the first to be developed. Nearly everywhere else that I have probed the Rocky Mountain Trench from Montana northward, it has been a funnel for transportation, agriculture, real estate, hydropower projects, and related activities. Here the view to both sides is, as it has always been, an embrace of free-flowing water, side-channels, and sloughs, with tall poplars and airy, white-barked copses of aspen fringing the wetlands and sandy-soiled meadows, and the rich bottomland habitats rolling gently and seamlessly away to become the curve of mountains that you know have ranks of other undisturbed valleys and mountains behind them.

Perhaps the rhythms of travel have unlimbered some old, vaguely familiar circuits. Or maybe I'm more exhausted than I realize. Whatever the case, I am overtaken by a strange yet comforting sensation, as though something that had been hovering around the edge of a slot finally dropped into place. Advancing down this green trough, through easy, sheltered topography that is every bit as untamed as the far snow-fields and cirques, I understand in my bones why the Ancient Ones came this way. It is the sort of natural passage any people from any era would choose. And all at once, I join every human migration, each foray to scout out what food or territory, splendors or salvation waits beyond the farthest landmark. Our small band is one more embodiment of the ageless, universal need to wander. I hear the footfalls of a cavalcade that extends back through time to our earliest forbears.

Though this place could scarcely be more removed from teeming crowds, it allows me to belong to humanity more fully than before. To think that there will always remain wild immensities in which we can venture when the mood strikes is a great solace. Such qualities in a landscape, like their power to engender waking dreams, are almost impossible to define. Yet they are surely among the most valuable resources preserved within the Muskwa-Kechika wilderness.

Then the dry benchland ends. We are hoisting ourselves over webworks of roots in the muck, searching for a way around some marsh lakes. For a while, we backtrack as often as we progress. When I ask Wayne if he has ever been lost, he answers, "No. There was that time Reed and I didn't know where we were for the better part of a week, but I knew how to get back where I'd come from. That's not lost." Which puts him firmly in the tradition of American frontier hero Daniel Boone, who also claimed to never have been lost, supposedly adding, "but I was bewildered once for three days."

When we find the stream we are seeking, it turns out to have been thoroughly reengineered by beavers. Travel now means pushing through head-high willow brush and plunging horseback through a seemingly endless series of ponds, much to the agitation of mergansers, goldeneye ducks, and their broods. Distances and days begin to blur. We gather horses, saddle and pack them, ride, hike, chop, trudge, unpack, gather firewood, pitch tents, try to dry clothing, eat, sleep, awaken, and start packing up once more as Wayne calls out, "It's a fine day for it."

"For what?"

"A very nice ride with some pain."

I like that better than when he says, "You'll have to put the whip to yourselves today, boys. That looks like some rough country ahead," because Wayne is never joking when he says rough.

All the while, we are gradually gaining altitude, penetrating farther into an outlier of the Muskwa Ranges. We could have stayed low, turning up the Gataga River, but its floodplain is so boggy between thick forest stands that a traveler would be tempted to just hole up and wait for the ground to freeze. The sidehills and scree slopes of the high country have become the more practical route.

Crossing an avalanche chute as we near the highest pass, the pack string comes to a sudden halt. Ray points his camera up into the brush while Wayne gesticulates toward those of us in the rear, clamping his hands together like jaws. Moments later, I make out a grizzly looking us over from a narrow ridge 100 yards aaway. This is not what Wayne and Ray have seen. But since they are watching another grizz, one which bolted uphill, they believe we are all pointing out the same bear. They continue to nod back unconcerned at my increasingly frantic signals.

About the time they get my message, the bear on the ridge settles down on the lip of its day bed and regards us with its head resting on its paws. If it were one of the hoary marmots whose burrows pock the slopes, the pose might be endearing. Plump and silvery-sided with long digging claws, these alpine rodents even look a bit like miniature grizz as they excavate wildflower roots. But instead we have a full-scale *Ursus arctos horribilis* taking our measure. When it stands up again, I notice that it has a lean, leggy look and long muzzle—traits often seen in young males, which are not my favorite grizz to happen upon.

Sure enough, the bear begins to approach, pauses for a better look, then keeps right on coming. Not only is it unintimidated by so many people and horses, it looks on the edge of being downright testy. We begin to holler, "Hey Bear! Ho Bear!" As we withdraw from the brush to a clearer part of the avalanche chute, I notice that the cow parsnip all around has been chewed and trampled and pressed down in bed-sites; we are smack in these grizzlies' favorite spot. The bold one makes a kind of half circle, regarding us out of the corner of its eye. Finally, slowly and somewhat reluctantly, it walks away down the drainage.

I have no trouble finding the energy to climb to the pass. After kicking steps up a last snowbank, I stand to catch my wind among dwarf forget-me-nots, buttercups, and gentians. Their petals glow with an intensity of color that is only partly due to the undiluted light of high altitudes. The rest, I suspect, has to do with leftover adrenaline, as the mountains falling away ahead and behind seem impossibly vibrant as well. At this moment, I know exactly how good it is to be alive.

We had planned to camp just before the pass. In deference to the bears, we continue a way down the other side before unpacking. I retrace the path to the top to bask in the sunset, whistling back at the marmots en route. After a few minutes, I decide to angle past cliffs to a ridge of rock flakes sorted by fierce winds and frost into striking designs emphasized by the fading, slanted light. The whole top of the world is turning the pink of tiny phlox and moss campion blossoms that cling to thin soil. A lone caribou walks the skyline to the south. There are Stone's sheep rams on the talus not far from it. Well below us, in the shadows, a thin plume of smoke rises from a waiting campfire.

Several days later, we are at Wayne's trapline cabin at the edge of a lake near the Gataga River. Just in time. Some of the horses were getting played out. A couple pulled in lame. Having come the last stretch too tired to walk but too rain-soaked and cold to sit horseback, I don't have a lot of bounce left in my legs either, so I wander by arm power, paddling Wayne's canoe.

A pair of resident loons with a baby claim one end of the lake. While beaver swim from shore to shore, some other furry object the same size keeps bobbing in place. I can't figure out what it is—until the rest of the moose emerges beneath that shoulder hump, dripping plant stems. More moose and a band of caribou feed along the western shore framed by the peaks we wound among to get here.

IF MY TRIP seems brief next to the itinerary of Wayne and Marcie, theirs pales beside the undertaking of a 30-year-old Canadian named Karsten Heuer. He left Yellowstone National Park in 1998, bound for Whitehorse in the Yukon Territory, 2,100 miles away, by foot, cross-country ski, and canoe. On the afternoon of August 10th, 1999, as I'm reading a book by the lake and feeling a zillion miles from anywhere, two strangers and a dog come strolling up, having swum the Gataga River and found the path to the cabin. One is Karsten. The other is Leanne Allison, who joined him partway through his epic trek, intended to help publicize the Y2Y Conservation Initiative.

"Down in the southern part of Y2Y, it wasn't unusual to do 30-kilometer [18-mile] days," Heuer says. "Up here, we're pretty happy to cover half that distance. This was a cool, late spring. We've hit a lot of snow in the mountains, and the late runoff has made for interesting river crossings."

"Some of the supposedly small streams have been all we could handle," Allison agrees, and ticks off the other rigors of the northern miles: Boggy ground, bugs, blowdowns, bears. I nod. I know. Before Heuer reaches Whitehorse, he will have muscled his way over a total of 100 mountain passes but crossed only five railways, 10 paved roads, and 55 fences since Yellowstone. That summarizes the potential of Y2Y. First, it is a continental stronghold for wildlife, which needs freedom of movement for its own genetic diversity and long-term survival;

second, it is one of the great reservoirs of nature left in the world. But the fact that Heuer will find all but 28 of the 320 drainages on his route marked by logging roads, seismic lines for oil and gas exploration, and other intrusions underscores the need for a large-scale plan.

Mired in political debate over conservation issues at the start of the 1990s, the British Columbia government divided its land base into large sections, then invited all the competing users in each to sit down together and hammer out their own Land and Resource Management Plan—LRMP for short. The process was spurred along by the government's 1993 announcement of a Protected Areas Strategy aimed at safeguarding 12 percent of B.C.'s total acreage in provincial parks and ecological reserves by the year 2000.

Along with the upper Kechika in the Rocky Mountain Trench, Wayne's trapline cabin lies within a 16-million-acre area covered by the Mackenzie LRMP. Its human population stands at fewer than 7,000, 94 percent of whom live in the village of Mackenzie near the southern end of Williston Lake. This LRMP already includes Kwadacha Wilderness and Tatlatui Provincial Parks. Additional sites proposed for full protection could effectively expand the Muskwa-Kechika wilderness. If negotiations go the other way, those same tracts may leap instantly into the machine age. During the latter part of our trip, we rode through timber flagged for possible cutting by bright strips of tape and galloped down the bulldozer trails of a potential lead and zinc mine.

Between wholesale preservation and wholesale invasion waits a third path intended to sustain both resource industries and the natural fabric of the Rockies—an alternative that was a key to Muskwa-Kechika. To learn more about how that 11-million-acre domain was established, I made a side-trip with Wayne before we broke camp at Denetiah Lake. We flew northward up the Rocky Mountain Trench to a lodge on the edge of Scoop Lake, where the Muskwa-Kechika advisory board had gathered. It was my kind of meeting, held in a saddle shed with everyone sitting on planks around a wood stove.

THE NORTHERN THIRD of British Columbia hosts only about 40,000 people. None of them farm, mine, drill, or log in the Muskwa-Kechika bush. Hardly any even live there year-round. Brian Churchill, a wildlife biologist and coordinator of the advisory board, told me, "That means we still had all kinds of room to try new approaches." Fifty roadless drainages' worth of options, to be more precise. "We brought a whole bunch of different people with different visions together. They already had experience working through the LRMP process. One thing they all agreed upon was that the old way of doing things, with each economic interest group pursuing its own single-use agenda, has got to change."

In the U.S., designated wilderness is off-limits to development, period. Guidelines for Muskwa-Kechika permit some industrial activity, though only in the special management areas. The reserve is still termed a wilderness because, in the words of the formative legislation, "the long-term objective is to return lands to their natural state as development activities are completed."

Most everyone agrees that cooperation between resource agencies helps maintain the integrity of ecosystems. Instead of merely hoping for this, the shapers of Muskwa-Kechika built in a provision that no one resource department can hand out development permits until all others with a direct interest have signed off on the plans. Roads for a project must be gated to prevent public motorized access during the period of operations. Afterward, the roads and development site are recontoured and put back as close to the natural condition as possible.

This strategy of integrated management over a large landscape in place of competition and piecemeal development came in good part from the man happy to settle for "a very nice ride with some pain." Wayne Sawchuk grew up in a family of loggers in Chetwynd, B.C., a timber center along the Hart Highway. He earned his living skidding sawlogs through the woods. Yet when the Ministry of Forests announced plans to cut the LeMoray drainage south of Chetwynd, he and number of other loggers opposed them. And won.

"LeMoray was just too beautiful, and it was the last pristine place around," Wayne said. "The trappers were with us. They know marten and wolverine are the first to go when the forest is lost. Hunters joined the fight too, because the moose get shot out when roads go in. Recreation is not as big a deal up here as it is farther south. What's driving conservation are people who hunt and trap."

Wayne stayed in the logging business another three years before shifting to work as a hunting guide all over the northern terrain. He first came to the Gataga River in 1985 with his uncle, who had a trapline there. Three years later, Wayne bought the trapping concession from him and began to explore the Muskwa-Kechika region. "I saw what the wildlife is like in an unspoiled ecosystem," he told me, "and I thought: why take on the logging industry and oil and gas companies one valley at a time? Let's get out ahead and protect the biggest, wildest section of countryside left." George Smith of the Canadian Parks and Wilderness Society was thinking along the same lines. Sawchuk and Smith formed the nucleus of what became a unique 20-organization coalition that included groups such as the Sierra Club, World Wildlife Fund, and B.C. Wildlife Federation, as well as hunters, trappers, guide-outfitters, and the Fort Ware First Nation. They proposed forming the Muskwa-Kechika wilderness from segments of three different LRMPs.

Darwin Cary and his wife, Wendy, who run Scoop Lake Ranch, have the exclusive guide concession for *Continued on page 154*

THE NORTHERN REACH
MAJOR ISSUES

Bleeding mineral wealth, a mountainside runs red with oxidized metals as springs seep through ore-bearing strata. This zinc deposit, near Braid Creek in northern British Columbia, is one of several known mining prospects in and around the Muskwa-Kechika wildlands. Development is prohibited on about one-third of this new reserve's 11 million acres. Limited mining and logging may be allowed in the rest, but only with provisions to maintain the area's overall backcountry qualities.

THE NORTHERN REACH

While a mining claim-post (above) marks a mineral deposit near the edge of Muskwa-Kechika, Wayne Sawchuk (right) prospects for a route through recently designated Denetiah Provincial Park, one of several reserves set beyond industry's reach. Carrying out a 250-mile expedition across the northern Rockies, this trapper, wilderness guide, and conservationist asks rhetorically, "How many places can you ride for three months without hitting a road?"

Moonlight, mosquitoes, and members of the Muskwa-Kechika advisory board gather on the shore of Scoop Lake in the Kechika River bottomlands. Participants include hunting and wilderness outfitters, spokesmen from logging and other industries, and members of First Nations—as local Indian tribes refer to themselves. They come to fine-tune a novel formula for satisfying the needs of people and wildlife so that the ecological integrity of this enormous landscape will remain not merely intact but world-class. After all, Muskwa-Kechika's moonlight also falls on an estimated 800 grizzlies, 750 black bears, 900 wolves, 1,500 mountain goats, 7,000 Stone's sheep, 4,000 caribou, 15,000 elk, and 22,000 moose.

THE NORTHERN REACH

Many a hubcap has gone spinning along the Klondike Highway, ultimately finding a home in this collection (right, top) near Five Finger Rapids, on the Yukon River. Many a gold-fevered would-be millionaire has raced through this country in a dogsled, canoe, or worn pair of hiking boots in search of the Klondike lode. And not a few bears have been lured to various town dumps (right, bottom) that always seem to accompany civilization's arrival. Yet even now some three-quarters of the Yukon Territory remains roadless backcountry, and towns like Dawson (opposite) still feel like outposts in a frontier that has never really yielded to settlement.

For some folk, conserving wildlife is a luxury. For First Nations people like Slavey Dene fisherman

and guide Floyd Moses, it guarantees full stomachs at home and sustains ageless cultural traditions.

nearly 4,000 square miles in the heart of Muskwa-Kechika. "I've got 20 people working for me," Darwin said. "That makes me the second biggest employer in Watson Lake. We're blessed with all kinds of wildlife for a simple reason—no road access. If we have a wildlife problem right now, it is too many wolves, in my opinion. There are 28 packs just between our area and the next guide's territory."

The mayor of Fort Nelson, Harry Clarke, told me, "The advisory board's goal is that all the values of Muskwa-Kechika will be here 100 years from now. If we manage so that any are wrecked, then what are we doing calling ourselves planners? I want my grandkids to be able to come out when they have kids and enjoy the things that I enjoy today."

Certainty is what the oil and gas business is after too, according to Rob McManus, who represented the Canadian Association of Petroleum Producers during negotiations over Muskwa-Kechika. "We were tired of battles," he said, "especially partway into a project, and tired of the bad guy image. With the Muskwa-Kechika proposal, I could go back to the industry and say look, we're not getting shut out; we just need to identify significant targets around the margins of the protected zones and settle on a management plan."

Finally, and perhaps most important over the long run, Beaver, Dogrib, and Dene Indians all have traditional territory in Muskwa-Kechika. They may be granted outright ownership of a substantial share once pending land claims are settled. Because they directly depend on living resources such as the caribou and fish, First Nations people largely approved of the wilderness plans, and the advisory board includes several Native American members.

THE KASKA TRIBE of Dene say Swan made the world by dropping feathers as he flew high above. One of the first feathers became a grizzly bear, and this is why Grizzly is considered a grandfather of all other animals. Speaking in his native tongue, Dennis Porter of the Kaska Dene Lower Post First Nation said that his own grandfather is buried near a lake not far from Scoop Lake and that his spirit is still living here.

"I want to see that this vast land maintains its beauty," Porter continued in English. "God knows, we have made enough mistakes. When we clearcut, we take away the animals' blanket, ruin the underground world. The days of cut-and-run are over. For stability, we have to call upon traditional knowledge as well as technology."

Later I spoke with Brian Wolf, whose mother has been chief of the Prophet River Band of the Dene Tsaa Tse K'Nai First Nation for three decades. He told me that some of his group's elders could foretell the future; Prophet River was named for one of them. They put up symbols to mark places where, in times of trouble, people could go and survive.

"All those places were in the Muskwa-Kechika area," Brian said.

In many ways, this wilderness is the result of a convergence of wisdom new and old. I leave it during the second week of August and fly to Muncho Lake, hop in a car, and roar north along the Alaska Highway past Liard Hot Springs. Every two hours or so, I cover the same distance that I did by horse and foot in two weeks, and I absorb almost nothing except landforms stroboscoping past the windows. In the morning, short on sleep and numb on the backside, I pull into the village of Teslin in the southern Yukon Territory.

Waiting by a float plane is Juri Peepre of the Canadian Parks and Wilderness Society. With him are resource experts and volunteers who plan to gather field data from a lowland expanse considered a potential candidate for national park status. After flying northeast to Wolf Lake, the expedition will canoe the Wolf River to the Nisutlin River, then paddle through its delta and across Teslin Lake back to the village. I am invited to come along in the small kayak that Juri brought. My skills in such craft are minimal. On the bright side, minor rapids provide me with all the thrills that hotshots have to seek among haystack waves and boat-slurping holes.

Out at Wolf Lake, I am practicing not capsizing when I notice with envy a nice, fat, roomy, stable, inflatable kayak on the beach. Next to it is a tent with a tarpaulin porch, and beneath that is a white-haired man frying a big lake trout over a fire. Adolf Metzler, of Duisburg, Germany, began coming to Canada to float rivers 20 years ago. After sampling the eastern provinces, he discovered Yukon Territory and has been exploring its waters on annual vacations ever since. Now age 69 and retired, he reached Wolf Lake nearly two weeks before our crew and will remain long after we are gone, then will descend the river alone.

"Always I travel by myself," he says, looking off toward the Pelly Mountains. "I like to be in the country and see the animals. I fish. I have wood and water. I take what I need. This free life in nature, I say it is a fever. Once you have this fever, you have it forever."

I move on to the lake's outlet. Wolf tracks run along one bank. On the other, Dave Jones is fishing for grayling. A grizzly bear expert who works as a land manager for the Gwich'in Tribal Council of Inuvik in the Northwest Territories, he is on loan to Peepre's survey team. While he repeatedly casts without a nibble, an osprey fishing just downstream makes three trips overhead, each time packing a good-size grayling.

Through the clear water, I make out a four-foot-long chinook, or king salmon, cruising next to some grayling like an aircraft carrier among patrol boats. One of the first arrivals of the autumn run, this salmon has come 1,400 miles up the Yukon River system from the Bering Sea, looping through the greater part of Alaska. Fasting the whole time, it burned its own tissues for fuel, gradually metamorphosing from a round-hulled, silvery giant to a lean survivor as purplish red as the huckleberries on shore. It has just enough strength to compete for a mate, scoop out a nest in the bright gravels below, and spawn. Then this magnificent voyager will die. Yet its decomposing body releases a wealth of organic material into these generally nutrient-poor headwaters, bolstering the food chain upon which developing fry depend.

Before it can carry out any final acts, however, Marty Strachan catches the chinook in a net and clips tissue from the gills, then releases it. In addition to making a general reconnaissance of the area's fish, he is after salmon DNA to help his employer, the federal Department of Fisheries and Oceans, identify the Wolf River stock. Jumping in to assist him is Ryan Clark, a 17-year-old high school student and member of the Teslin Tlingit (pronounced Klinkit) First Nation. Intent on broadening his outdoor experience after years of living in a city to the south, he was selected to join the team while doing summer work in a territorial conservation program.

I N THE NIGHT, rivers of fire burn among the constellations and run down across the still surface of Wolf Lake. The warm-weather display of northern lights keeps me up a long time, and departure day dawns too soon. We launch the boats. Within a few hundred yards, we are bouncing and scraping among thickly scattered boulders. Luckily, summer is far enough along that the Wolf is neither very fast nor deep. But the rock garden lasts all day and into the next. The only time the canoe teams are able to quit yelling "Left! Now Right!" "Hard Right!" "$%#@*&!," and the like is when the scientists pull ashore to gather information.

As Strachan and Clark wade to corral salmon, Jones takes the opportunity to patrol the shoreline and adjoining woods, searching for grizz tracks, droppings, or rubbing trees. Bruce Bennett, from the territorial wildlife department, disappears to collect plants. Chances are this avid botanist will have extended the known range of several species and found one or two rare ones before he returns. If a bird wings by or merely calls from the bush, he will quickly identify it as well, adding to the record of fauna the team is building.

As for myself, I keep close count of the number of hops during the stone-skipping contests held at pull-outs. Challenges are hurled. In fact, trash is talked, and the athlete representing a glorious superpower nation immediately to the south is disrespected. Strictly in the interest of keeping sports fans informed, let me just report that, despite fielding all but one of the entrants, Canada manages to lose the First Wolf River Invitational Hydrodynamic Rock Fest. Better luck next time, eh? Ya rubber-armed hockeyheads. Harrrh.

Downriver, I swap vessels to join Minnie Clark in a canoe. Born into the Dakl'aweidi (Eagle) clan of the Teslin Tlingit, she has fished and camped in parts of the Wolf River drainage, and wants to see more of the landscape. Clark works not only for the territorial fish and wildlife agency and the federal Department of Indian and Northern Affairs, but also for the Teslin Renewable Resources Council, established for the management of local renewable resources.

Teslin, she tells me, comes from the Tlingit word for "long narrow waters." People have long traveled upriver to hunt moose and trap beaver around Wolf Lake. In the heyday of Hudson's Bay Company trading outposts, some parties continued east across the Continental Divide and down the Liard river system to swap furs for goods at Fort Liard and even at Fort Simpson, hundreds of miles from Teslin.

Nearing the Englishmans Range, the river widens and slows and begins to take moosey turns with oxbow lakes—former channels—on either side like parentheses. The river's bottom is sheeted with bright sand. Solitary and spotted sandpipers forage along the bars. Each bend brings another belted kingfisher, and bald eagles appear every few miles. One remains perched on a branch that overhangs the water, closely inspecting each boat in our convoy. Then the current's pace picks up once more, and we go slaloming through new sets of boulders.

Peepre, who has traveled the Wolf before, signals for a stop and tells us, "You'll want to eddy out on the left shore up ahead." Miss the mark, and the cataract waiting beyond will permanently change the shape of your boat, head, and a few other items. In the forest, wild currant grows through the ribs of one of the heavy moose-hide boats abandoned here decades earlier by Tlingit hunting parties returning from Wolf Lake. We carry our light canoes around. Strachan provides lunchtime entertainment by launching himself in the kayak over a waterfall into the chaos of backwash and hydraulic funnels. His technique is astonishing, his courage unquestionable. As for the soundness of his mind, opinions vary. Perhaps only Peepre, who has paddled every imaginable kind of northland river, understands how Strachan is able to control his own fate in such a tumult.

Riding the rapids below the cataract in open canoes feels risky enough. Already heavy with extra gear, Dave Jones and I take on so much water we can barely maneuver. Bruce Bennett and his partner flail away high-centered on a rock, their boat revolving like a helicopter blade, before dropping back into the current. Now Peepre signals to eddy out on the right shore. No one waits an extra second to respond. The maw of jagged stone across the channel tops a waterfall that would grind our whole show into fish chum.

Like the Davie Trail along the Rocky Mountain Trench, the portage route through these woods has probably been in place for generations beyond counting. No doubt the caribou had a good trail tramped out before that. Their droppings are the most common big animal sign throughout the Wolf River drainage. Pellets practically pave the drier sites, where lodgepole pines rise above a silver carpet of the lichen called caribou moss, a staple winter food for these northern deer.

Of the 23 major woodland caribou herds in the Yukon Territory, only two or three are in habitats not yet fragmented by human activities or subjected to wolf-control programs. One is the Wolf Lake herd, numbering around 1,500. These animals and the intact bottomland forests and riparian range showcased here help explain why the sweaty gang hauling baggage along the portage trail includes Doug Harvey from the park establishment branch of Parks Canada.

"We have 39 national parks," he tells me. "A large share are in scenic mountain country and the Arctic. Some years ago, our emphasis shifted to making sure we protect an example of each biogeographic region. We need 14 more parks to complete the system, and one of them should represent low-elevation northern forest." Since Parks Canada does not want to proceed without local support, Harvey approached the community of Teslin with the idea of a Wolf River park in 1997.

"Most Tlingit people are interested," Minnie Clark informs me. "But there is concern that a park might interfere with hunting and trapping." Indigenous groups are guaranteed the right to carry on traditional subsistence activities in all of Canada's northern national parks. Some locals are not aware of this. Others are, but mistrust the government.

To find out what the majority want, the Teslin Renewable Resources Council is conducting a door-to-door survey of all resident adults during the time of my visit. The question is not whether to declare Wolf River a park. It is only whether Parks Canada should launch a formal study of that possibility. Such a phase would last at least two years, Harvey says. If the findings are favorable, planners still will have to work out policy details and legal boundaries. He has seen national parks become a reality within seven years. The usual time is closer to ten years, and twenty years is not unheard of.

No matter; once declared, parks are for the ages. Aren't they? We now understand that to truly last with their full complement of species and natural processes, reserves must not become cut off from the larger ecosystems around them. The Y2Y Conservation Initiative looks toward securing the necessary connections. These early efforts to fashion a network of protected areas along the backbone of the continent are bound to be labeled impractical, touch off controversy, and yield disappointments along with successes. Whatever the case, it is fascinating to be among people trying to figure out how to save the wildest of wild communities and freest of spaces for generations yet unborn.

Someone asks Peepre if he feels that discussions over the fate of a certain stretch of countryside elsewhere are getting realistic yet. "I hope not," he answers. "Otherwise, we will have failed. Sometimes I think we need a whole new paradigm in the Yukon. Not more little green dots of parks but a commitment to keep the majority of the north free of roads and development." Of course, there are plenty of people who would call this not a vision so much as a nightmare—a blockade of progress. Human habitation and commerce will almost certainly expand through the wild north country. To what extent? Is major transformation inevitable? Desirable? In which direction does true progress lie?

Peepre's special interest at the moment is winning protection for three spectacularly wild tributaries of the Peel River: the Wind, Snake, and Bonnet Plume. Were they in the lower 48 states, each would be a buzzword among outdoor adventurers. Running through the northern end of the Mackenzie Mountains, they are as little known as their futures.

The South Nahanni River, at the southeastern end of the Mackenzies, is a different story. Its canyons—Canada's deepest, enclosing hot springs, whirlpools, and Virginia Falls, nearly twice as tall as Niagara—became Nahanni National Park Reserve in 1972. After skiing down part of this Northwest Territories waterway in winter, I floated it in summer and was so smitten that I turned around and ran much of the river again. And again.

Near the lower end, I ventured from First Canyon up onto the Ram Plateau, a karstland where rainwater falling onto a soluble limestone formation carries a little more of the earth away down sinkholes and underground rivers with each storm. The cliffs I climbed were honeycombed with caves. As I squeezed down into those tunnels, the light from my lamp exploded across ice crystals and frozen blue layers, as though I had uncovered winter's secret lair. Outside in the summer air, caribou and bison roamed deep, sudden valleys hidden from the outside world almost as completely as the caves.

The Ram Plateau is immense, and the news is that it will probably be added to Nahanni Park. One day, I may paddle the Wind, Snake, or Bonnet Plume, too. I might go on to trek by the mineral-colored crags of the Tombstone Range. Or wander any of a hundred other rivers and chains of peaks waiting in the far northern reaches of Y2Y. For now, however, I am more than content to drift lazily from the Wolf toward the Nisutlin River bottomlands, whose lakes are havens for nesting trumpeter swans.

In the delta, which is dappled with smaller waterfowl and already protected as a federal wildlife reserve, Bruce Bennett points out a cluster of willow twigs. Cut by beavers upstream, they washed down to lodge on this mud flat, took root, and have begun growing again to feed the beavers and moose of a new neighborhood. Nature's workings remind me of her rivers, infinitely changeable, endlessly renewed. Ashore, I enter a tall forest of poplar, aspen, spruce, and pine. These woods could be almost anywhere between the Yukon Territory and Yellowstone. So could the mountains that ring Teslin Lake. And so, for years to come, could I. North or south, a few miles from town or weeks into the bush, this is the country I call home. ◆

FOLLOWING PAGES:
MUNCHO LAKE PROVINCIAL PARK
Mirrored finish of this park's namesake lake all but obscures the fact that, at far right, the Alaska Highway shoulders into its shoreline in northern British Columbia. Higher up, clouds and sunlight chase each other across slopes where bands of Stone's sheep and mountain goats dwell, often visible from the roadside. This park is both part of the huge Muskwa-Kechika wildland complex and a gateway to backcountry in almost every direction.

DAVIE TRAIL AND BRAID CREEK

Grizzly graffiti: Ripped tree trunk along Davie Trail (left)—may be a signpost on which the great bears use four-inch claws to exchange information about ranges and social status. Homing in on human scent, a silver-tip (right) pauses in digging up an avalanche meadow near Braid Creek, in the Muskwa Ranges. Such slopes, snow-scoured during winter, often grow thick summer crops of cow parsnip, spring beauties, and avalanche lilies—all prized grizz groceries.

FOLLOWING PAGES:
MAYFIELD LAKES, MUSKWA-KECHIKA

Widespread hoofs help woodland caribou distribute their weight, serving not only as winter snowshoes but also as summer bog stompers in northern muskegs and marshes. This trio finds refreshment at a mineral lick near the Gataga River.

MUSKWA-KECHIKA
Sunset brings a surreal glow to remnant snows on a pass through British Columbia's Braid Creek Mountains (left). Near the skyline of the northern Rockies, the difference between an evening hike and a vision quest can become minimal, as landscapes nurture communion with the soul.

FOLLOWING PAGES:
RAM PLATEAU, N.W.T.
With infinite wilderness overhead, a traveler's tent lit from within turns into a starship navigating the northern lights. Contrary to a widely held belief, the aurora borealis is not strictly a phenomenon of winter nights in the Arctic. It paints summer skies as well, and can occur as far south as Yellowstone.

SOUTH NAHANNI RIVER

White plumes and rainbowed mists spring from the South Nahanni River at Virginia Falls (above), nearly twice Niagara's height. Its Athapaskan name means "powerful river," and it has carved Canada's deepest canyons (right), replete with whirlpools, eerily eroded pinnacles known as hoodoos, and hot springs that help make it the centerpiece of 1,840-square-mile Nahanni National Park Reserve.

FOLLOWING PAGES:

DEATH LAKE

Nestled amid the Nahanni karstlands, stunning Death Lake owes its name to its reputation for being too short a runway for many a bush pilot.

NAHANNI KARSTLANDS

Testament to mishap, a Dall's sheep skull in Igloo Cave (opposite) is all that remains of the animal after its head became wedged in the ice-floored crevice long ago. Other caves hold sheep thousands of years old, frozen solid in accumulated ice as if on display inside glass. Soluble limestone layers raised from the bottom of ancient seas compose the extensive Nahanni karstlands, which rain and meltwater have sculpted into a wonderland of arches, sinkholes, and other formations (left, top). Marine fossils such as this ammonite (left, bottom), a long-extinct relative of the modern nautilus, abound.

FOLLOWING PAGES:
IGLOO CAVE

Gardens of flowerlike ice crystals bloom in Igloo Cave, encouraged by still air and constant temperatures to grow over the long term.

NORTH NAHANNI
Textures of the tundra:
Winter staple of caribou,
the lichen commonly
called caribou moss sur-
rounds a sprig of crow-
berry (below). Curvaceous
blades of curly sedge
(opposite)—one of a
group of northern plants
adapted to marginal
conditions—may also
become caribou fodder.

FOLLOWING PAGES:
RAM PLATEAU
Staircase for titans,
a canyon leads ledge by
limestone ledge up to the
scenic Ram Plateau. Such
evocative topography of
the Nahanni karstlands
may soon become part
of Nahanni National
Park, ensuring protection
for this section of the
Mackenzie Mountains.

RAM PLATEAU

Highs and lows here range from tundra tablelands (left) to the Ram River's scoured canyon (above). While trappers, traders, and gold-seekers probed much of this northland early on, explorers did not penetrate its great canyons until the 20th century. Even now, the Nahanni backcountry offers few clues as to which century it is in.

FOLLOWING PAGES:

TOMBSTONE RANGE

Tombstone Mountain takes on prism-like qualities after an early snowfall. Near Y2Y's northern end, the Tombstone Range—part of the Ogilvie Mountains—has become the Yukon's newest territorial park.

NISUTLIN DELTA

Golden opportunity for the Tlingit people who live here, autumn brings seasonal gatherings of waterfowl to the Nisutlin River Delta (left), part of a new national wildlife area in Yukon Territory. Wolf River (above), a tributary of the Nisutlin, boasts an intact herd of woodland caribou and is being studied for possible inclusion in Canada's national park system, which allows subsistence hunting and fishing by native peoples. Should it win park status, it would add one more vibrant gem to Y2Y's long necklace of priceless protected areas.

YUKON TERRITORY
Victory marks the face
of Karsten Heuer (and
perhaps Webster, too)
as they end their epic
two-year, 2,100-mile
trek just south of the
town of Teslin, on
the Nisutlin Delta. At
the local school, Heuer
presented a slide show
explaining the Y2Y
Conservation Initiative
and its strategy for
keeping things wild in
the continent's wildest
heartland—yet at the
same time seeking to
preserve local commu-
nities. In the Rockies,
healthy landscapes go
hand-in-hand with
tourism, recreation,
robust wildlife popula-
tions, and environmen-
tally sound industries;
such diversity holds
the promise of a sus-
tainable economy—
rather than yesterday's
boom-and-bust cycles
with their legacy of
depleted and degraded
resources. Day's-end
view of a wetland
reserve on the Yukon's
Nordenskiold River
(opposite) warms the
soul if not the body.

EPILOGUE

IT IS LATE AFTERNOON of an October day, cool in the woodland shadows, warm as I reach the edge of a hillside clearing and sit facing the sun. The light has that autumnal heft that makes it seem to stick to everything it touches, hazing it with gold. Exactly where this is doesn't matter too much except that if I were to climb one of the fir or tamarack trees, Rocky Mountains would emerge all along the skyline.

Tufts of summer-cured orchard grass in the meadow below glow with the same aura as the elk bedded among them. There is deer sign all around me. More elk appear every so often on the clearing's far side. I came here to listen to them bugle when evening draws nigh. Until then, I have the staccato voices of squirrels in the background and the notes of pine siskins harvesting luminous seedheads from thistle patches. A coyote trots partway into the meadow, sniffs along the length of some fallen logs, and places its front feet up on one to nose the breeze. Suddenly, it flicks its ears lower and retreats alertly toward a thicket of serviceberry brush. Three ravens lolling around on cushions of warm, rising air follow the coyote's progress along with me, commenting to one another all the while.

Coyotes and ravens are among my favorite creatures, as they were for many Indian tribes, partly because both species survive by their wits and partly because of the quality of that intelligence. These beasts are inventive. I think they are capable of insight, or reasoning. I think they possess a sense of themselves and even a sense of humor. I think we talk about, try to manage, and determine the fates of a great many species as though we know a lot about them when we have only a rudimentary, myopic understanding of what they really are. The Indian view of coyotes and ravens as loquacious talkers, tricksters, and creators comes closer to the essence of these beings than does all the dry mechanics of western behavioral science; I would wager any amount of autumn gold on that.

Certainly there is a fortune of the stuff at hand. Every slender willow leaf, every cottonwood canopy, is gilt and glittering. The aspen copses are a curious alloy: Some trees gleam solid gold, while others shine yellow most of the way up but smolder pink or orange toward their crowns. A bronze hue radiates from the serviceberry brush. The dogwood shrubs run to burgundy. I don't really care whether the elk bugle or the resident wolf pack swings by. I like this setting just as it is. I belong to it. I won't wish for a single thing more when I go.

When I was last here, this world was an infinite variation on green. It looked green, felt soft and green, smelled green through and through. Except that off toward the meadow's far corner was a pool of crimson. Startling but not harsh. Blood-red but nothing to do with claw or fang. It was a solid mass of tall poppy blossoms by an old cabin site.

Though the building had long since rotted away, the flower clump had spread and continued to bloom every summer out in the wilderness. Before homesteaders arrived, the same meadow probably held seasonal encampments of Salish or Kootenay Indians. To one degree or another, we humans have been part of the Rocky Mountain scene for a long time. But people used to dwell within the framework of their environment; today no one knows whether we will be able to do that in the future or will end up knocking the framework apart.

Months later I find myself on the outskirts of Mexico City, at a meeting of jaguar experts from South, Central, and North America. I am a long way from Y2Y, but not all that far in many respects. The western hemisphere's largest cat prowls from northern Argentina to northern Mexico and occasionally on into the southernmost United States. Like most big predators, it is under pressure from hunting, poaching, and control actions to protect livestock. And like most big animals in the world today, it suffers from the rapid loss and fragmentation of its habitat amid a burgeoning human population.

This is the first time the jaguar biologists have ever gotten together. Their purpose is to pool their knowledge and come up with a general conservation plan. References are made to *Paseo Pantera*—the Panther's Route, a possible north-south movement corridor outlined years ago for mountain lions, whose range is also pan-American. But to stay healthy, both cougars and jaguars will need more than travel routes. They must have protected living spaces with good prey populations along the way. How large? How close together? As the discussion turns to what an effective network would look like, several scientists bring up the Yellowstone to Yukon Conservation Initiative as a model.

Along similar lines, the Northwest Ecosystem Alliance has long advocated managing the vast Columbia River basin of the Pacific Northwest as a single, indivisible watershed. Recently, faced with the impending extinction of the Columbia's salmon, the federal government authorized its resource agencies to do just that—to treat the entire Columbia Basin as one ecological unit from the Rocky Mountain headwaters to the tidal flats of Washington and Oregon.

Have you heard about R2R, someone asks? No? Well, he explains, it's a proposal for a bridge of wildlands extending from the Rockies to somewhere on the Pacific Coast that begins with the letter R. M2M? A habitat linkage along the Mississippi River heartland from Missouri to Minnesota—or is it Michigan? The Algonquin to Adirondacks conservation strategy, A2A, addresses the eastern U.S.

And then there is supposed to be Big A2A, an Arctic to Antarctic plan.

Most such notions are still in the back-of-an-envelope-sketch stage, only a step or two beyond rumors passed hopefully from one enthusiast to the next. While they can seem pure pie-in-the-sky, they do open the arena for much-needed debate, just as the Y2Y Conservation Initiative does. Is it really so impractical to imagine a web of interconnected natural areas crisscrossing a nation, or even a number of nations? What if this were the most practical way to keep natural systems functioning? What if it proved to be the only way?

That appears to be what modern biology is telling us. It is why Florida has moved to establish greenways linking natural areas throughout the state. And why there is a Tropical Andes strategy for connecting parklands in different countries sharing the western Amazon Basin. And why cooperation between Kenyan and Tanzanian reserves is crucial to the Serengeti ecosystem, and why authorities are inventing ways to let wildlife move more freely among the parks of four next-door nations: South Africa, Mozambique, Zimbabwe, and Botswana.

Whether the concern is elephants in the southern African thornveld, koalas in Australian forests, or wolverines in the Rockies, the solution lies with maintaining the integrity of large natural areas and the bridges between them—and doing so before things reach crisis stage. The emphasis is on preventive medicine rather than treating an ever-lengthening line of patients.

Like captive-breeding programs for endangered species, the parks and reserves set up in North America represent a stopgap measure originally begun in reaction to market hunting and the wholesale transformation of landscapes by westward expansion and the industrial revolution. Except for wildlife refuges acquired along waterfowl flyways, there was nothing particularly systematic about these efforts at protection. Supporters scrambled to set aside what they could where they could—which usually meant places that no one else had much use for. It is tempting to draw parallels between island-like wildlife parks and the reservations set up for native people and ask how much of the intent was to save the inhabitants and how much was to conveniently isolate them and get on with affairs.

Over the years, ecology became a recognized field of science, then a household word. Advances in animal behavior, genetics, and population dynamics changed the way we view wild communities. Yet we continued to go about preserving nature in pretty much the same way, species by species and place by place, often only after they were confronted by some threat. At last the focus is shifting, now that planners comprehend that trying to save species without providing for the ecosystems in which they are embedded is ultimately a sterile exercise.

Early in the 1990s, a cadre of North American conservation biologists and activists began what they called the Wildlands Project.

Mapping out the continent in terms of its major biotic landscapes, they are identifying huge blocs that they feel should be devoted primarily to sustaining biological diversity. These are concentrated mainly in the wildest places left, where open spaces and public lands prevail. But the blocs also include some settled countryside with a welter of economic uses. In many of these areas, Project spokespeople suggest, human activities should be scaled back in favor of nature's. Other areas could even be returned to their original condition—rewilded.

Critics promptly labeled this exercise the work of environmental megalomaniacs. But whatever else you want to call wishful thinking, it at least involves thinking, as opposed to merely reacting. You generate ideas, throw them into a free society, and see what happens. With luck, someone might translate one or two into a fresh enterprise.

Inspired by the landscape-level view of wild resources in the Rocky Mountain region, Harvey Locke, a Canadian lawyer now in Boston, took a lead role in putting together the Y2Y Conservation Initiative. He also has been involved in politics and, characteristically, is not given to understatement when speaking about his cause. "Coexistence with nature is one of the greatest challenges, if not the greatest challenge, of our time," he says. "During our civilization's push westward, we had this great concept of progress as obliterating nature, driving all that is wild before us to be replaced by a pastoral vision of European settlement. That ran into a barrier at the western edge of the Great Plains. The Rocky Mountains were not only a physical obstacle but so spectacular and spiritually overwhelming that they caused people like Theodore Roosevelt to re-think the frontier philosophy.

"Y2Y stands for the connections that will allow our diversity of wildlife to last over the centuries," he continues. "It also creates a diversity of economic opportunities for people, relieving them from boom-bust cycles of resource extraction by connecting them with the community of the Rockies. I was reading the other day about Paul Revere and the early days before the American Revolution. The movement was full of independent individuals from different walks of life. They had no common agenda except this powerful, powerful idea."

Powerful because of its simplicity: an inalienable right to life, liberty, and the pursuit of happiness. Now we have to figure out how to carry on without squandering the lives and freedoms and joys that arise from our natural surroundings. They are still there, still vital all the way up and down the Yellowstone to Yukon region. Forget the conservation initiative for the moment; ignore all the politics and opinions. Just see the country. Experience as much of the Rocky Mountains as you can. Somewhere here, you might find that the untamed core of the continent somehow fits inside you even as it towers and shines overhead. I don't know how or why, but I know it feels right. Once that happens, the way ahead will seem more and more clear. ◆

FOLLOWING PAGES:
OGILVIE MOUNTAINS, YUKON
The proverbial race is to the swift—like this cross fox, a color phase of the common red fox. Yet the race is also to the fluttering and delicate, as any painted lady butterfly proves. And to the breath-holding, workaholic beaver, the slow and steady mountain goat, the camouflaged ptarmigan, the enormity we call a moose, and the obscure little carrion beetle that will one day scavenge the carcasses of the others, recycling their nitrogen for plant roots to use. This is how biological diversity works in an intact Y2Y ecosystem: Everyone wins, including the humans who share this outstanding terrain with its incomparable wildlife.

INDEX

Boldface indicates illustrations.

NOTES/ACKNOWLEDGMENTS/ADDITIONAL READING

NOTES ON THE CONTRIBUTORS

Wildlife biologist **Douglas H. Chadwick** is the critically acclaimed author of *The Fate of the Elephant* and *A Beast the Color of Winter*, a perceptive study of mountain goats. In addition, he has written two other books for the National Geographic Society: *The Company We Keep: America's Endangered Species*, and *Enduring America*. A longtime conservationist, Chadwick spent seven years studying mountain goats and other wildlife in Montana's Bob Marshall Wilderness and Glacier National Park. He has published more than 200 articles and remains a frequent contributor to NATIONAL GEOGRAPHIC magazine. He lives with his family in northwestern Montana.

Freelance photographer **Raymond Gehman** specializes in outdoor and natural history subjects, and prefers northern regions, where life often seems most fragile. He has contributed often to NATIONAL GEOGRAPHIC and TRAVELER magazines, and to the Society's Special Publications, including *American Legacy: Our National Forests*, *Yellowstone Country*, *Exploring Canada's Spectacular National Parks*, and *Great Rivers of North America*. He lives in central Pennsylvania with his wife Mary Lee and sons Andrew and Michael.

ACKNOWLEDGMENTS

The Book Division is grateful to the many individuals, groups, and organizations that helped in the preparation of *Yellowstone to Yukon*. Special thanks to Y2Y stalwart George Wuerthner, who served as consultant; to Bart Robinson and Kat Wiebe, of the Yellowstone to Yukon Conservation Initiative; to Doug Harvey, of Parks Canada. Also, to outfitter Loyal Letcher, bush pilot Ted Grant, and Lyn Clement, for her careful reading of this book.

Author's acknowledgment: In addition to each and every person mentioned in the text, the author wishes to thank George Wuerthner for a close reading to check factual accuracy, Louisa Wilcox for background information and advice, Loren Kreck for inspiration, Paul Brown of TBC Lumber for perspective on the timber business, David Rockwell, Wayne McCrory, Mark Haroldson, Mark Bruscino, Art Soukkala, Troy Merrill, David Mattson, Len Ruggiero, Kerry Murphy, Doug Honnold, Bob Crabtree, Rob Ament, Mike Ivie, George Halmanza,

Mike McIvor, Peter Aengst, Martha McCallum, Shelley Alexander, Leah and Sylvia Gibson, Brian Horesji, Stephen Legault, and Timm Kaminski. Thanks of deeper order are due my family—Karen Reeves and Russell and Teal Chadwick—for the very best company a hiker could have in the bush—and my editor, Tom Melham, who made it ever harder for me to distinguish between work and pleasure throughout my journeys and the writing of this book.

ADDITIONAL READING

◆ Douglas H. Chadwick, *Enduring America* (National Geographic Society)

◆ Douglas H. Chadwick, *A Beast the Color of Winter: The Mountain Goat*

◆ Ben Gadd, *Handbook of the Canadian Rockies*

◆ Thomas McNamee, *The Grizzly Bear*

◆ James H. Pritchard, *Preserving Yellowstone's Natural Conditions*

◆ Ray Rasker and Ben Alexander, *The New Challenge: People, Commerce and the Environment in the Yellowstone to Yukon Region*

◆ Louisa Wilcox, Bart Robinson, and Ann Harvey, *A Sense of Place: An Atlas of Issues, Attitudes and Resources in the Yellowstone to Yukon Ecoregion*

Additional information on Y2Y can be obtained from:

Yellowstone to Yukon Conservation Initiative
710 9th Street, Studio B
Canmore, Alberta T1W 2V7
Canada
(403) 609-2666
Y2Y@banff.net
website: www.rockies.ca/y2y

Greater Yellowstone Coalition
Box 1874
Bozeman, MT 59717
(406) 586-1593
gyc@greateryellowstone.org
website: www.greateryellowstone.org

Composition for this book by the National Geographic Society Book Division. Printed and bound by R.R. Donnelley & Sons, Willard, Ohio. Color separations by NEC, Nashville, TN. Dust jacket printed by Miken Inc. Cheektowaga, N.Y.

YELLOWSTONE TO YUKON

By Douglas H. Chadwick
Photographs by Raymond Gehman

Published by the National Geographic Society

John M. Fahey, Jr. President and Chief Executive Officer
Gilbert M. Grosvenor Chairman of the Board
Nina D. Hoffman Senior Vice President

Prepared by the Book Division

William R. Gray Vice President and Director
Charles Kogod Assistant Director
Barbara A. Payne Editorial Director and Managing Editor
David Griffin Design Director

Staff for this Book

Tom Melham Project and Text Editor
Greta Arnold Illustrations Editor
Suez Kehl Corrado Art Director
Rebecca Beall Barns Researcher
Douglas H. Chadwick Picture Legends
Carl Mehler Director of Maps
Thomas L. Gray, Map Research and Production
Jerome N. Cookson,
Mapping Specialists
R. Gary Colbert Production Director
Richard S. Wain Production Project Manager
Lewis Bassford Production Manager
Sharon Kocsis Berry Illustrations Assistant
Peggy J. Candore Assistant to the Director
Dale-Marie Herring Staff Assistant
Kathleen Barber Indexer

Manufacturing and Quality Management

George V. White Director
John T. Dunn Associate Director
Vincent P. Ryan Manager

Philip L. Schlosser Financial Analyst

The world's largest nonprofit scientific and educational organization, the National Geographic Society was founded in 1888 "for the increase and diffusion of geographic knowledge." Since then it has supported scientific exploration and spread information to its more than nine million members worldwide.

The National Geographic Society educates and inspires millions every day through magazines, books, television programs, videos, maps and atlases, research grants, the National Geography Bee, teacher workshops, and innovative classroom materials.

The Society is supported through membership dues and income from the sale of its educational products. Members receive National Geographic magazine— the Society's official journal— discounts on Society products, and other benefits.

For more information about the National Geographic Society and its educational programs and publications, please call 1-800-NGS-LINE (647-5463), or write to the following address:

National Geographic Society
1145 17th Street N.W.
Washington, DC 20036-4688
U.S.A.

Visit the Society's website at
www.nationalgeographic.com.

Library of Congress Cataloging-in-Publication Data
Chadwick, Douglas.
      Yellowstone to Yukon / Douglas Chadwick ; photographs by Raymond Gehman.
            p.   cm.
      Includes index.
            ISBN 0-7922-7862-3 (reg.)   ISBN 0-7922-7863-1 (dlx.)
  1. United States and Canada—Description and travel.
  2. United States and Canada—Pictorial works I. National Geographic Society. 2. Title.

HE356.F63 2000
973.04'26   99-05957